# LUTHER'S ROSE

## About Highland Books

You are invited to visit our website <u>www.highlandbks.com</u> to learn more or to download our catalogue. We may also from time to time post errata there. If you wish to tell us of significant mistakes we invite you to e-mail us at <u>errata@highlandbks.com</u>.

# *LUTHER'S ROSE*

*A dramatised biography of
Katharina Luther,
née von Bora*

**Ursula Koch**

Highland Books

First published in German by Brunnen Verlag Giessen, under the title *Rosen im Schnee, Katharina Luther, geborene von Bora*

German original ©1995 Brunnen-Verlag Giessen

First published in English by Highland Books, 2 High Pines, Knoll Road, Godalming, Surrey GU7 2EP, England

English translation © 2003 Highland Books Ltd.

Translation and Editorial Notes: Norman J. Threinen, Edmonton,

Cover artwork © Thomas Vogler

ISBN  1 897913 53 2

Printed in Great Britain by Biddles Limited, Guildford, Surrey

# Notes on this English Translation

English usage is intended to be 'mid-Atlantic', avoiding the idiosyncrasies of either the USA or England.

The German original recreates the atmosphere of the times by using formal language and the occasional old-fashioned use of words and phrases. Similarly this translation avoids modern idioms. We have also used certain liturgical forms of the 1662 Anglican Book of Common Prayer (it conveys an atmosphere even though it was written over a century later than the events of this story).

We have in the main retained German spellings of proper names, and have retained certain Germanisms in the forms of address, which in general are more formal than in English; we have considered them as virtual parts of the proper names: So we have used Fräulein (instead of Miss), Herr (Mr or Sir), Herr Doktor (m'learned Sir?), Frau (Mrs), Frau Doktor (a polite form of Mrs when her husband is 'Herr Doktor'), Magister (professor), Meister (master craftsman).

Paragraphs set in italics are imagined thoughts of Katharina in the first-person.

# Wittenberg, February 20, 1546

*First the cock – and then me! That's the way it always was. As he crowed outside, I groped my way through the dark hall to the kitchen beneath.[1] The others were still asleep, all of them: the children, the maids, the students, the hired man – and he, my husband who had been lying beside me. I heard him snoring. It was not loud. It was almost a purring, like the cat by the stove. He didn't hear the cock. Nor did he hear the door as it creaked softly. Most of the time he slept until the dawn cast beams of light through the windows and the noise of the children penetrated his dreams.*

*True, he often dreamt, tossed about, bellowed like an ox. His dreams wrenched me out of deep sleep. When I slept, I was as one who was dead but when I awoke, I was instantly alive. I quieted him down and spoke softly as I stroked his chest with my hand. His chest rose and fell under the weight. Toward the morning, he slept.*

*I ran cold water over my arms and washed my face. Then I lit the fire in the hearth and awakened the maids. Sometimes someone was already standing at the door as I heated the milk on the fire – a beggar in rags, his face full of scars. We brought him in, gave him soup and a piece of bread. My husband in the bedroom continued to sleep. While the children got up and stormed out into the yard, he continued his restless sleep.*

---

*The cock crowed. Today as always, but he did not rouse me from sleep. I felt physically battered as if I had a fever. Long before the cock crowed, I got up, lit the lamp and sat on my bed in the flickering light. When I stretched out my hand, it touched only a cold, clean sheet. No one groaned in his sleep. There was no sound. No warmth. Thus began my new day. What should I do with this day?*

*The cold, winter wind whistles through the cracks. Nothing moves in the monastery.[2] Everything appears to be dead. The monastery. The city. Only the wind races through the streets. Just like yesterday, when the messenger arrived.*

*He came early. Almost no one would have seen him. He came through the gate, down the street in the wind and pounded on the neighbour's door. Then they came to me – three men, their heads bowed.*

*Why was I so startled when they knocked on the door? Did we not often receive guests, early or late, friends or strangers, nobles or beggars. Why then was I seized with such foreboding?*

*"I fear that if you do not cease your anxieties, the earth will finally swallow us up ... ," he had written from Eisleben. How he had reviled me for my anxiety! As though I lacked trust in God. Fortunate is he who trusts in God at a time when weapons are being sharpened and pyres are burning everywhere. It may well be that God intended it for good for him, for me – as He did with our Magdalena, our child whom He took from us. But I am only a poor woman who has great difficulty understanding the councils of the Lord. I am anxious. "What does it change?" he had said. Nothing. Nothing.*

*I know. Yet I would dearly have liked to wring another precious year from our heavenly Father with my anxiety and my prayer. Must it then be now? Already? Herr Doktor[3] still had so much to do. The whole world cried out for him. He had to travel here and there, to settle disputes and to proclaim the Word. In the middle of winter – with no concession to his advancing years. It is still too soon for him to go. For me, it is too soon. The wind whistles around the house, whistles through all the cracks.*

———————

*Our friends came and knocked at the door. The house echoed under the blows. Wolf[4] hobbled to the door. When I saw them and Philip put down his black collar, I did not even have to ask. I stared into his darting eyes, at his twitching mouth, at his hands which tugged uneasily at his coat.*

*None of my sons were with me. I drew Margaret to myself, the only one still with me in the dark house. I acted as if I wanted to protect her, while I myself needed protection. I dared not open my mouth.*

*Finally Wolf asked, "Do you have a report from Eisleben?"*

*"Yes."*

*"From Doktor Martinus?" No answer. Then I said it. Again, I had to be the one. No one had the strength to say it. "Has something happened to our master?" Philip nodded. "Is he not well?" Again, no answer. "Is he dead?"*

*His arms fell. His lower jaw dropped. I no longer saw him. I only heard the screams of the maids. Wolf tried to support me. Margaret threw her arms around me. Only the walls stood firm as always. He is dead. Doktor Martin Luther is dead.*

*The friends remained with me, sitting silently around the table. It was quiet in the house. At noon, I asked them to leave. I wanted to be alone and tried to pray. But I only sat at the window and waited for it to nightfall. Nor did I find rest during the night. I was with the messenger as he travelled, bringing the report to villages and cities, carrying it from hearth to hearth, in cottages and castles. He is dead. Foes rejoice; friends wail. And what about me – his wife? What should I do now? Who am I? What remains for me now?*

*"Get up, Katie," he would have said. "Get up and thank God that He has redeemed me. Go to your work, Katie! God is with you in all that you will do. Stir yourself, Frau Doktor! Jump to it, Madam Merchant! There are still people to whom you can give orders, Sir Katie!"*

*His voice – never again? The bed beside me – cold, empty? I am so afraid, so ... It seems as if I should return ... Go back into the convent.*

# Nimbschen, 1509-1523[5]

The large, dark gate, covered with black iron, slowly opened, but only a crack. A little girl, dressed in a bright dress and wrapped in a long cape, stood there and did not move. Her father shoved and pushed her forward with his hand until she almost fell as she finally took a step through the narrow opening. Her father following had to squeeze through with greater difficulty. Out of the grey mist of the yard in front of them, a white figure came towards them.

The little girl turned and stumbled against her father. She felt the coarse fabric and the cold metal of his belt. "Herr von Bora?" With a sound of reluctance, the man pushed the child away from him. He took her small hands into his own. Then he pulled his daughter behind him over the pavement which was wet from the rain. The nun who had let them in disappeared into the house on the left beside a long building near the entrance. Herr von Bora shifted impatiently from one foot to the other. The clammy air felt heavy on his head, which buzzed from a night of drinking. He remained near the gate which would lead him back outside. Only him. But, almost imperceptibly, the little girl strained in the same direction.

In the light spring rain, a few days after Easter, the outer yard of the Throne of Mary convent seemed to be washed clean for the visitors. From the stables came the sound of restless horses. The colts strained to get outside. But their attendants kept the animals locked up. Even the cattle remained in the shed awaiting the last blast of winter. In the Mother Superior's once-elegant living quarters which had deteriorated somewhat over the centuries the doors were firmly locked. From the choir loft of the church on the other side of the yard one could hear the sound of the nuns chanting.

"Go on in." The nun who answered the gate pointed to the door of the house. "Our Reverend Mother will receive you after she has finished praying Vespers." Darkness again. The little girl was pushed up some stairs. Her father groaned behind her. A new door opened. The child felt the dampness of her clothes and sat down by a hearth where the coals still glowed from a fire which had just gone out. The nun left the visitors alone. The father paced to and fro with heavy steps. Floor boards creaked. His lips quivered. The little girl noticed it but waited in vain for him to say something. She drew her thin cape even tighter around her upper body and listened anxiously. Finally they heard voices. A hushed murmuring came closer and then became more and more faint. Footsteps. Doors closing. The creaking of stairs.

"Get up!" The child stood up slowly. Her father remained standing. The door opened, letting a blast of cold air into the room. As she came in, the Reverend Mother pushed aside her veil and turned to Herr von Bora with furrowed brow: "We expected you earlier, Cousin Hans. Is this your daughter Katharina?"[6] She apparently did not expect an answer but spoke to the nun accompanying her. "Bring the little girl into the dormitory, Sister Barbara! Where are her things?"

Katharina pulled a tightly bound bundle from under her arm. The abbess nodded. She stretched out her right hand and grasped the little girl's jaw. Katharina looked through a veil of tears into the cold blue eyes above her. Her small mouth did not move. With a soft sigh, the woman released the child's head and stretched out her ring finger. "Kneel down," whispered her father. Katharina bent down obediently over the ring and kissed it. "Say goodbye to your father," ordered the abbess. Herr von Bora screwed up his face. He gave the little girl his hand and turned away. Katharina stared at her father's back.

"Come in, Cousin Hans. We still have a few things to arrange. I have heard that your second wife has provided you another little girl. So, your sons have another sister ..." Following the abbess, Hans von Bora left the room through a small door. Katharina followed the nun. At the stairs, she turned around once more. But Sister Barbara had the ring of keys in her hand already and rattled them impatiently. Katharina stumbled down the stairs. Outside, the overcast day had become dusk. She clutched her bundle to herself and tried to keep up with the hurried steps of the white figure ahead of her.

---

"What is your name?" "Katharina. And you?" "Elsa." "Be quiet. You should be asleep," the occupant in the next bed hissed. In the dark dormitory, the students of the convent lay tightly side by side. Outside the rain fell noisily.

After a while the quiet breathing seemed to signal that their comrades on the right and left were sleeping. Another whisper: "How long have you been here already?" "At Easter it was two years." Katharina sighed. "It is only difficult at the beginning," whispered Elsa. "I cried a lot, too. But you must not show it. You must be proud. After all, you will be allowed to learn something. Are your parents rich?" Katharina hesitated. She had heard her father cursing as he opened his wallet in which he kept his gulden.[7] "I don't think so." "Then be content. If you're not rich, you wouldn't get a man anyway." "Oh, be quiet. Why do you say such dumb things?" "Sleep well," murmured Elsa and turned over on the other side.

Katharina pulled the thin blanket over her shoulders. She was cold. In Brehna, it had been warmer and there had also been a fire in the hearth in the dormitory. But her father had come right after

Christmas and taken her out, complaining that the happy sisters were greedy.[8] Then, in the manor, a new wife. Katie's brothers called her "mother" and mocked her when she tried to discipline them. But Margaret, the old maid, had wrapped a fleece around Katharina's cold feet. Katharina did not want to cry, absolutely not. But no one could see her. And starting tomorrow she would be brave like Elsa and all the others. Starting tomorrow …

------------

*"Pastor, pastoris."* – the pen flowed across the paper with a light squeak. "The shepherd!" A fly buzzed around over the bowed heads of the girls. It was still cool in the high vaulted room where the students in the convent were being taught. But outside between the walls, one could feel the warmth of summer. The farm animals were in the pasture. As Katharina looked up, she could see out into the open air through a crack. Clover blossomed under the sun and, as if in a dream, a sheep stood motionless with its lamb in the middle of the meadow. The shepherd!

In summer, great herds of sheep used to graze in the pastures surrounding the old farm of the von Bora family and the children loved to go out into the middle of the herds. The boisterous boys had fun with the timid animals. But Katharina, the youngest von Bora, who should not even have gone out with her high-spirited brothers, loved to hold the small lambs in her arms. And the good-hearted shepherd showed her the very young lambs which were still so soft.

"Katharina. You are dreaming!" Sister Gertrud raised her rod threateningly. Startled, Katharina pulled herself together. Ashamed, she put her head down over the Latin words. Sister Gertrud never actually used her rod; she just swung it through the air. One could see in her face that she and the rod did not belong together; that she only had it there because she thought she should. In spite of this, Katharina listened to what she said. Otherwise the eyes of the sister showed a hurt which the girls could not bear. They loved Gertrud even though they had difficulty putting the Latin words on paper or pronouncing them. "*Agnus*" – "the Lamb." Katharina forced herself to sacrifice the image of the soft skin of the young lambs and their tender moist lips for Sister Gertrud.

"*Agnus Dei*" – But if Jesus was Himself a lamb, is a person then not permitted to love the lambs in the pasture. Like the old shepherd. Will he come again this year? His beard would certainly have grown still longer. And his hat had large holes which must really be unpleasant when it rains. "Katharina, where are your thoughts today?" Sister Gertrud looked with concern at the paper full of ink-spots. "Can't you write just a bit more carefully? You have blotted a whole herd of sheep." Katharina did not have to answer. The bell called them to prayer.

———————

Between the columns of the high nave of the church, the little girls in their grey aprons stood close together while the clear voices of the nuns praised God from the choir loft. Katharina waited impatiently for the ringing of the Angelus bell. For the songs were in Latin and she understood only the odd word. *Lauda, anima mea, dominum: laudebo dominum in vita mea* ... Finally, the bell rang which proclaimed the approach of the angel to Mary.

"*Ave Maria, gratia plena* ... " Her lips moved, "Hail, Mary ... " This she could already pray, along with the pious women who sat hidden behind the choir lattice. Katharina imagined that heaven began there. The nuns sat on luminous clouds, a golden light over their heads. She imagined Sister Gertrud who sang with a pointed mouth, closed eyes, and a lot of enthusiasm.

However at the same time, Sister Adelheid, who had hit little Margaret so hard yesterday, also came to mind. Margaret had not really been disobedient. She had only picked her nose. Katharina forgot the clouds and heaven and looked anxiously at her finger. As long as something like that didn't happen to her. For Sister Adelheid used her rod to strike the hands of the children. And that hurt – not only the hands. It hurt right to the heart and Margaret had cried for a long time yesterday.

The second ringing of the Angelus bell roused Katharina from her thoughts. No, it could not be the same in heaven as in the choir of nuns. She sighed.

In the semi-darkness of the church, her eyes moved backwards and forwards between the bare columns. Elsa, who stood beside her, poked her side with an elbow and whispered, "Did you hear that? That is certainly Sister Elisabeth singing off key." A quivering voice rose from the choir above the others and stopped. The echo died away in the vaulted ceiling and the cantor began anew. Katharina's gaze remained on one of the columns. She no longer heard the singing. A beam of light fell on the Madonna in the south aisle of the nave. The Madonna had been donated to the convent by a pious friend only a few weeks earlier. Mary wore a crown and beneath it a veil almost enwrapping her. The child on her arm seemed to have moved somewhat away from his mother's body and was reaching with outstretched hands into the darkness of the nave. He was laughing and seemed to enjoy himself while his mother directed a very serious look toward the side of the altar blocked by the choir lattice. Katharina looked carefully at the face of the Virgin in the limited light which fell upon it. It was round and proportionate and more beautiful than anything Katharina had ever seen. But her mouth seemed to sigh. Her head was bent somewhat as if it bore an invisible weight. Despite this she held herself upright. It certainly could not be the child which was too heavy for her. It must be something else.

The Madonna's long hair fell freely across her gown. The girls were never permitted to show off the beauty of their hair. Every woman was to conceal beneath a scarf or veil what a man might find attractive. But not Mary. Was it God who permitted Mary to show her hair? For, she certainly wanted to please Him alone and no one else.

Katharina came to with a start. The "Amen" faded away between the columns. The most impatient of the girls were already pushing towards the side door in a hurry to get to the dining hall where soup was steaming in large kettles. Katharina was being pulled along. But as she went out, she looked back again. Could the Holy Virgin perhaps move? Could she not give little Katharina a sign? But from the portal, the Madonna was in the shadows.

In the evening at Vespers, Katharina slipped into the church ahead of the others. She approached the column with a pounding heart, stood on tiptoe and tried to look directly into the face of Jesus' mother. Mary's eyes were bright from the light which streamed into the nave through the rose window above the west portal. Katharina searched and searched for words to say. But nothing came to mind except "Mother" and again:

"Mother, you are so beautiful.
Here take your child, Oh beautiful mother!
Delight in it forever, you lily, you rose."

Imploringly, she raised her hands and searched the stony face of the statue for an answer. Suddenly she felt something heavy on her shoulder. She shivered. "How lovely that you should pray to our beloved Lady. Do you know how the verse continues?" Katharina shook her head without speaking.

"May your chaste hand,
Nurture the body of this newborn.
Give your child your breast.
For he needs you on this earth."

Sister Adelheid smiled at Katharina and then vanished into the choir room. "He needs you on this earth," Katharina repeated softly and then again more bravely aloud. At that moment it appeared to her that the M`other of God smiled at her. Behind her, the portal opened. With quiet whispers, the school girls pushed their way into the church under the care of a lay sister. In the choir, the garments of the nuns rustled. Vespers had begun.

---

"Katharina, Katharina, the cat has kittens." Elsa and Margaret stumbled through the garden and dragged their friend by the apron across the convent yard. In the corner of the cow shed sat the black and white cat. She mewed anxiously as the little girls drew closer. The three girls sat down around her and tried to calm the mother cat. However the confusion of their voices made the animal still more anxious. "Be quiet," said Elsa to the others. Quietly, the girls waited until the mother cat allowed them to look at her blind, naked offspring. "How small they are!" "We are not allowed to touch them yet." "What shall we call them?"

"So, you have discovered something," laughed George, the young hired man, behind them. He carried a sack in his hand. "Out of my way. I will take them away."

"Take them away? Where to?"

The young man laughed again, loud and rough. "Into the pond, of course." He pushed the girls who had not moved roughly to the side and bent down over the nest. The cat leaped at his arm and scratched it, drawing blood. "Damn animal!" With extended claws, she prepared for a new attack.

"You can't kill them," shrieked Katharina. "I can't?" said George, taken aback, his mouth open. "Well, why not?" "But they are ... " At a loss for words, Katharina looked at Elsa who hung her head. "No, you can't," declared Margaret resolutely and began to cry. Katharina reached out her hand to the little one.

"Get away!" With a mighty blow, George sent the desperate mother cat flying toward the wooden wall. Stunned, she fell into the straw. Then he bent over the kittens, picked up two at a time and tossed them into the sack.

"No!"

"Yes," he taunted. "You wouldn't want to bring up all of them, would you?" He threw the wriggling sack over his shoulder, took a menacing step toward the cat who approached him again, and stomped out of the barn.

Stunned at what had happened, the children stared at the empty pile of straw. Katharina looked at the cat walking around them mewing softly.

"I would have fought harder for my children," she said reproachfully.

"I don't want any children!"

Margaret wiped her tears with her apron. The girls stood up and walked slowly across the yard. Half way across, Katharina turned. "I will tell Mary!" And she ran to the church. Shaking her head, Elsa looked after her.

Under the statue, Katharina knelt on the cold stone floor and wept. "He wants to drown them. Holy Mother of God, help them. Help them live." The south aisle of the nave lay in the shadows. The stone statue was lifeless in the darkness. "Do something, beloved Mary. I will – I will ..." She couldn't think of anything to promise the Mother of God. She stood up and looked around lost for words. Everything was deadly quiet. "If I was a mother, I would not permit it," she said to Mary and stamped her foot. Mary remained upright. Only her head was slightly bowed.

––––––––––––––––

"Katharina!" "Psst!" "*Magnificat ...* " sang the nuns in the choir. "Katharina, did you hear? Elisabeth will marry." "Marry?" The impertinent Elsa received a poke in her back and dropped her head again in devotion. "*Anima mea dominum.* "

Katharina studied the slim back of Elisabeth as she stood in front of her. She was a head taller than most of the school girls but otherwise she was no different than they were. "Marry?" thought Katharina and tried to imagine what it would be like. She recalled her boisterous brothers. They would also some day take wives for themselves. She did not know if she should envy or pity these future wives of her brothers. She recalled the maids screaming as they ran away from the hired men and in the process lifting up their dresses so that one could see entirely their naked legs.

At the evening meal where, according to the Cistercian Rule[9], the school girls were to listen in silence to someone reading – but they were not always quiet and Sister Gertrud appeared to be a bit hard of hearing – Katharina asked Elsa quietly between two spoons full of cabbage soup, "So, who will Elisabeth marry?" Elsa shrugged her shoulders and eyed the table of the sisters. "I don't know exactly. I believe it is a Duke of Mansfeld. He is quite old already."

The first group of girls carried their dishes into the kitchen and hurried out into the open air. It was a warm late summer evening. The students were permitted to speak in the yard. Even the hired men raised their voices there and the sheep bleated in the barns. Katharina and Elsa sought out a quiet nook under the projecting roof of the sheep shed.

"I heard it from fat Anna. Anna heard it from Gisela." "And no one asked Elisabeth?" "No. But, have you not seen her face? She walks around as though she was being sold to the Turks. Yet, thereby she will become a duchess and have beautiful clothes. She will be able to eat what she wants every day and not always have to fast and her maids will dress her every morning." "Do you really believe that?" Elsa was quiet. She didn't really know what it would be like to be married. "I can imagine it would be nice," she finally said emphatically. "I don't know," said Katharina.

A couple of weeks later, as the harvest was already in full swing and the wagons of the farmers rumbled through the gate entrance loaded with the fruits and vegetables which they were obligated to give to the pious women, a small coach pushed through the maze of people and animals. The driver who sprang from it pushed the curious farmers' wives aside and strode to the house of the abbess.

The school girls stood at the doors and windows of the school building even though Sister Adelheid waved her rod through the air. None of the girls moved to return to their desks. With open mouths, they stared at the slender horses and the beautiful coat of arms which adorned the doors of the coach. Elisabeth stood among them. Furtively the girls looked at her. She was pale but did not move. A servant of the abbess came running across the yard and whispered a message to Sister Adelheid. The sister laid her rod on her desk and called, "Elisabeth!" Elisabeth turned around obediently, walked to the sister and bowed her head. Adelheid placed her hands on her for a moment. Her lips quivered, then she turned and Elizabeth went with the servant to the abbess. A short time later she reappeared in the yard wrapped in a bright cape in spite of the summer heat. The hired man carried her bundle. He also helped her get into the coach. She did not look back. The wagon turned and raised a cloud of dust. It disappeared through the gate entrance.

"Return to your seats," ordered Sister Adelheid, her voice quieter than usual. As Vespers began, Katharina folded her hands and blinked over at the Mother of God. "Protect Elisabeth from all harm, Holy Virgin, as she must now marry." She felt a shiver go down her back. "*Supplices te rogamus omnipotens deus ...* " "Humbly we pray to you, almighty God."

---

All Saints Day was barely over and the wind began to blow rain and snow through the windows. The girls were shivering as they sat over their books. They drew their thin garments more tightly around themselves. Their red frost-bitten hands could hardly hold the quill pens any more. More and more slowly they formed their letters and words. More and more often their work was interrupted by sneezing and coughing. "*Miseratio hominis circa proximum ...* " "The compassion of man is toward his neighbour ..."

Winter came early that year! Margaret, who sat next to Katharina, suddenly laid down her quill pen. Her entire body shook in a coughing fit. Katharina turned to her. "Write on!" commanded Sister Adelheid. "*Misericordia autem Dei ...* " "But the mercy of God ... " Margaret tried to continue writing. She couldn't. She gasped for breath. "Go into the dormitory and lie on your bed," said the sister. As she stood up, the child tottered. "Katharina, go with her." Katharina took her frail friend tightly by the arm. They had to proceed slowly, step by step. Margaret's hand was warm and twitched. In the yard, it was already dusk. A late farm wagon rattled over the stone pavement.

In the dormitory, Margaret threw herself down on her bed without a word and groaned. Katharina stood beside her, not knowing what to do. "I'm freezing!"

"Wait, I'll get you some blankets." Katharina was glad to be able to do something. She grabbed blankets from the beds of the others. But after she had wrapped them around Margaret, the girl screamed loudly, "Give me water! Water!" Katharina ran to the well, came back breathless, and brought the cup up to the lips of the sick girl. Margaret shivered. The water ran over her chin and on to the blanket. But she sighed and sank down satisfied when the cup was empty.

It became dark in the dormitory. Katharina looked anxiously out at the overcast sky. She was afraid. "Katharina!" Her sick friend stretched out her hand, seeking her help. "Stay with me!" "I will stay with you. You can count on it. Don't worry." Katharina shivered from the cold but did not move from the bed of her friend, even when she seemed to have fallen asleep. A bell summoned them to Vespers. She heard the others cross the courtyard, moved her lips and tried to pray the Psalms: "*Domini, probasti me et cognovisti ...* " (O Lord, thou hast searched me out and known me ...)

Finally, as they finished praying in the church, the voices of the sisters and the other girls drew near. Katharina saw the flickering of their lamps above the wall. Sister Adelheid and Sister Gertrud came to the bed of the sick girl accompanied by a nun whom Katharina had never seen before. Behind them, the girls scurried in but Adelheid ordered them roughly to go and eat their meal. "You were right to stay with your friend, Katharina," said the stranger softly and kindly to her. Her face was bright in the glow of the lamp. She had friendly eyes. "I am Magdalena von Bora, your father's sister." She shook Katharina's hand and then bent over the sick child.

Amazed, Katharina studied her aunt of whose existence she had been unaware. But from deep within her subconscious, she remembered: her father walking through the room with heavy steps; she sitting by the hearth; someone raising a protest. "My sister also went," said her father. "Magdalena also went into the convent at the age of ten."

"I will get herbs and boil some tea," said Magdalena after she felt the sick girl's pulse and hot forehead. The child looked trustingly at her but then had another coughing fit. "Come with me, Katharina." Sister Gertrud remained behind at Margaret's bedside with the lamp. Katharina stumbled across the dark courtyard behind Sister Magdalena. The wind blew snow flakes toward them. Suddenly they were in front of a small door. Magdalena opened it and stepped into the interior of the convent. Katharina held her breath. She hardly dared to cross the threshold. In front of her she saw only the shadow of the nun. The nun felt Katharina's hesitation and turned around. "Come, you don't need to be afraid. Leave the door open. You will soon be going back out again."

A few steps brought them into a vault filled with wonderful smells. With a steady hand, Magdalena lit a lamp which shed light on the walls where hundreds of plants were hanging. Beneath them sheaves lay on shelves. Glasses filled with seeds or leaves stood around and a big book lay open in which Katharina recognized precise drawings of leaves and roots. "This is the pharmacy, Katharina," said the nun. "Here the pharmacist sister prepares everything which we need to help the sick." She carried the lamp into a corner and worked there with some glasses and leaves. Katharina remained standing in the darkness and waited. A fire burned in a small stove. Magdalena brought some water to a boil and poured it over the prepared herbs. Katharina inhaled deeply: a smell of balsam filled the room. "Could we not bring Margaret here?" she asked softly. The nun turned to her and stroked her head sadly. "No, Katharina, here we are only permitted to nurse the sisters who live with us under enclosure. Sister Adelheid will care for the girl.

Take this jug to her! I will accompany you with the lamp as far as the door."

Katharina took the jug with the warm boiled mixture tightly in both hands and followed the nun. At the door Magdalena turned back: "You will now find your way!" Katharina heard the door latch. She groped her way cautiously in the darkness. The light of a lamp in the dormitory showed her the way. Sister Adelheid nodded to her as she reached the bed of her friend. Carefully they administered the tea to the sick girl.

Margaret coughed all night. In the morning, a bit of light broke through the grey clouds. The sick girl dragged herself to the window. Katharina was allowed to stay with her. At noon another school girl, Anna, also lay in bed with the fever. A couple of hours later, Veronica joined them. Katharina hurried from bed to bed. Sister Magdalena was again called from the convent. At Margaret's bed, she shook her head sadly. In the afternoon, Margaret coughed blood. The sisters carried her into a small room where a fire burned in a hearth. They called the priest. Margaret was burning up with fever. Father Bernhard came and anointed her with oil. As Katharina awoke the next morning, she heard the girls say to one another in a hushed voice, "Margaret has died."

The sisters dressed the child in a white garment and Katharina picked a couple of asters which were still blooming by the wall. She put together a bouquet and slipped it under the folded hands of her friend. Two hired men carried the dead girl over into the church and the choir of nuns sang the requiem mass. "*De necessitatibus meis eripe me, Domine ...* " "O bring thou me out of my troubles, Look upon my adversity and misery ... "

---

Winter came to an end. In the cemetery beside the grave of Margaret, five additional graves had been chopped out of the frozen earth by the hired men. Lilies-of-the-valley now blossomed on the hills. A lukewarm wind blew across the cemetery and the birds twittered their spring songs. The nuns maintained silence during Lent while the buds on the branches of the trees filled with sap and life. With the end of the Easter celebrations, the countryside turned a fresh green while schoolgirls and nuns decorated the church and altars to prepare for the Pentecost festival.

Sister Adelheid supervised the girls. After the evening meal, she called Katharina to herself. "Come along to the clothes cupboard!" While Adelheid searched, Katharina looked around her and asked, "Why do I need new clothes? My old ones are not yet torn." "No," said Adelheid and looked at Katharina disapprovingly. "You have not torn them but they have become too tight. And watch out that you do not soil your bed. Here are a couple of clean rags. Lay them under you when you sleep. When they get soiled, wash them. "

Katharina took the rags and later showed them to Elsa. "Do you know why I should lay these under me?"

"So that you do not soil your bed."

"But I don't soil my bed. I am not a small child anymore."

"But it happens to women too," said Elsa.

In the darkness on her bed, after she had removed her outer garment and the new aprons and had folded them carefully beside her bed, Katharina felt her body with her hands. She was shocked. She had become fatter.

"Elsa."

"Yes."

"Elsa, have you also become fatter?"

"What do you mean, fatter?"

"I mean your breasts."

"Yes, certainly. It happens as you get older."

"Only to women?"

"Yes, only to women."

Elsa yawned aloud and turned on her other side. Katharina stared into the darkness perplexed. She thought of the Virgin Mary and suddenly remembered a picture at home – in the church – not far from the manor: There the Holy Child lay in the arms of his mother and drank from her breast. If Elsa had not been breathing so deeply and been so quiet, Katharina would have asked her whether Mary also had to use rags.

During the night, Katharina dreamed about Elisabeth who was now a married duchess. She dreamed that Elisabeth like the mother of Jesus had a child at her breast and that she looked very happy. The next day at Morning Prayer, she stole a look at the Mother of God but she no longer dared to ask the question which came to her during the night.

---

Katharina drew the golden thread through the cloth and began a new stitch. She sat with Ave and Anna on a bench and stitched with them on an altar cloth. At the other end of the room, Sister Adelheid sat with the younger girls, bent over a simpler pattern.

"Have you heard about Sister Gertrud?" whispered Anna. "What?" "She is no longer allowed to teach." Katharina sat up. "Why not?" "She is being punished." "How do you know that?" "Be quiet and work!" Sister Adelheid ordered the girls. They dropped their heads again. But Katharina got the new stitch wrong. She looked enviously at Ave's skilful hands which moved much faster than hers. Her fingers felt clumsy and thick, much too plump for such a fine thread. She put down her needle and looked outside. Yes, if she could only go out into the garden. But it was raining. Several drops of rain fell with a loud noise on the stone window sill and into the room. The damp, cold air made it feel chilly in spite of the fact that it was summer and the harvest was underway.

Sister Adelheid came over to inspect the work which the girls had done. Katharina raised her needle, pressed her lips together and stitched on. "Your stitches are much too large – way too far apart, Katharina! You must make smaller stitches! Naturally it takes longer. You have no patience." If only the sun was shining, thought Katharina, then I could weed in the vegetable patch. "This is holy work," Adelheid turned to the three girls. "You should encourage yourselves with prayers and Psalms!" "*Psallite domino qui ascendit super caelos caelorum ...*" (Sing praises unto the Lord, who sitteth in the heavens over all... ) Obediently, Anna continued, " *... ad orientem, Alleluia.*" ( from the beginning. Alleluia.)

As Adelheid returned to her place, Anna began anew: "Evidently Sister Gertrud was disobedient."

"I can't imagine that," whispered Ave.

"You *are* allowed to pray your Psalms more loudly," Adelheid called over. *Ascendit deus in jubilatione ...* (God is gone up with a merry noise and the Lord with the sound of the trump ...)

"She is no longer allowed to leave the enclosure and must do the most menial work."

"How do you know this?" whispered back Katharina. Anna moved her head from side to side.

"People pick things up." She distorted her small mouth and added with the air of an initiate,

"We are dealing with a strict order! After all we are in a Cistercian monastery."

Katharina was silent while the others mumbled on with the Psalm. She heard the rain rustle on the window, her thoughts full of sympathy about Sister Gertrud.

*Yes, the Black Nuns back there in Brehna were not as strict. You would often hear them laugh, indeed sometimes very loudly. The convent stood in the middle of the city – unlike the Throne of Mary which was set far out in the fields and meadows. When the doors of the school in Brehna opened in the morning, girls streamed noisily in from the houses of the patricians in the surrounding streets. The rooms were adorned with wood panelling and there were cushions on the benches. Here – here everything was made of stone, cold stone.*

Katharina's hand moved across the columns at which she sat. Above her the vaulted ceiling was supported by slim, unadorned pillars. 'This is not our home,' Sister Gertrud once said, 'therefore our Father Bernhard[10] ruled that we are only permitted to build out of cold, grey stone. However, in heaven you will see colours, colours … ,' and the face of the nun had radiated great joy.

Katharina let go of the columns and looked again at the embroidery in her lap. *Sister Gertrud was right. My home is not here.* Katharina von Bora had no home; she had to wait until God opened heaven for her. And there, yes, there was her mother ready and waiting for her, arms outstretched and joyfully calling: 'Come, my little Katharina, come!' And her mother would look just like the Virgin Mary in the church, with long uncovered hair and a white veil.

Katharina sighed so loudly that Ave looked up. She laughed softly: "You certainly didn't get very far, Fräulein von Bora!"

"Oh, I just can't do it." She tugged at the thread and it tangled. A knot developed which was still there when the bell for Morning Prayer sounded.

"You can help in the laundry room tomorrow," said Sister Adelheid as they left the room. Katharina breathed a sigh of relief.

---

At last the sun was shining again! Its heat became trapped between the walls as the farm hands brought in the hay. Sister Adelheid was waiting for Katharina in front of the school building. "The Reverend Mother wants to speak to you." She checked out the child's clothing. Katharina had just come out of the garden. She had tucked in her dress and had pushed up her sleeves. Her arms were sunburned. Her face was covered with dust. Dusk was falling but she had gone out again after Vespers to finish preparing the bean patch. On a day such as this she did not want to go indoors too early. The cherry trees were hanging full of red fruit and the smell of summer flowers filled the air.

"Put on a clean apron and wash your face and hands." Shaking her head, Adelheid went away. Katharina walked to the well. Pulling up a bucket of water, she bent down over the dark entrance to the well. Suddenly, as she looked down into the mirror of the water, she saw a friendly face, flushed from being out in the sun. It was no longer the face of a child with large eyes and full cheeks. It was the face of a young woman with high cheekbones, alert eyes and a narrow mouth. Shocked, she fell silent. The water spilled out of the bucket and erased the picture in the mirror. Katharina took the bucket from its hook and set it down.

Very little light came through the window's bottle glass, as Katharina waited in the consulting room of the abbess. A servant of the Domina, a term which the sisters also used to address her, brought a lamp and set it on a black table. Finally, the Reverend Mother came in, a letter in her hand.

"Sit down, Katharina." She laid the letter under the lamp on the table, straightening it with her hand. "Katharina, I have received news that your dear father – after having been provided with the comfort of the holy church – has died. Your brother, Hans, has taken over the estates and will divide them with your father's other sons. "

Katharina sat motionless on the chair. She stared at the paper, the seal, the signature of her brother. In the background she saw the lime tree in the yard in front of the farmhouse and the heavily engraved door which led into the dining room. She heard the clamour of her siblings and the voice of her father leading his horse from the stable...

After a pause, the abbess said, "Your father brought you to us when you were ten years old. Now you are fourteen. It was his wish that you should consecrate your life to God in faithful prayer." Katharina heard the words as though she was hearing rustling leaves in the garden. She saw the small door in the wall through which she had once accompanied her aunt Magdalena; she pictured the rood screen in the church (though now she no longer imagined heaven lay behind it); and she heard the reverberation of the nuns singing in the vaulted chamber.

"Are you listening to me, Katharina?" "Yes — No — I am confused. Forgive me, Reverend Mother." Suddenly the woman's facial expression changed. With a quick movement, she reached for Katharina's hands and pressed them sympathetically. "Listen to me, my dear child. I am a cousin of your dear mother[11] who died before you spoke your first word. Your father didn't know what to do with you. You have no one in the world out there. And you are poor. No other convent will accept you unless you are able to bring a good piece of land, a village or a bag of money as a gift. I want what is best for you."

"I know." Katharina bent over the hands of the abbess and kissed them. "You are very good to me."

The Domina leaned back and rolled up the letter. With a firm voice she said, "So, you will go into the sisters' house tomorrow. You will study the rule of St. Benedict and you will follow all the ordinances of the novitiate director."

"Yes, Reverend Mother."

"Then, go!" [12]

Katharina stumbled down the stairs as she had when her father brought her. She walked across the courtyard into the dormitory of the school girls. The others sat on their beds and talked with each other. They waited for the clock to call them to Vespers. Katharina sat down and listened to their conversation. Elsa had not been with them for a long time. A couple of weeks earlier, Ave and her sister had left the school house and had disappeared behind the tightly locked door of the big house.

"Why are you so quiet?" asked Lena who had come to Throne of Mary only the day before Pentecost.

"I am going to be accepted into the enclosure tomorrow," said Katharina more to herself than to the others." With open mouths, the little ones stared at her.

"So soon?"

The following morning, Katharina shook the straw mattress on which she had slept and spread a fresh sheet over her bed. After Morning Prayer, while the other girls followed Sister Adelheid into the classroom, she went alone across the sunlit yard to the convent building which was attached to the south wall of the church. Several hired labourers, their farm tools over their shoulders, came toward her and grimaced. "Look, the gracious Fräulein is also going to work already," they taunted. Katharina looked at the ground. Between the rough hewn stones of the pavement, young grass pushed out into the light. She allowed a thick black beetle to crawl by her feet. She looked over at the school building and at the barn on the other side of the yard. And then she watched a singing lark flying up into the sky on the other side of the wall.

Katharina did not stop until she got to the door of the house. She knocked and waited. With a soft muttering sound, an old nun opened the door to let her in. From the glaring light of the summer morning, Katharina stepped into the shadow of a high vaulted room. She heard the heavy bolt shoved in front of the door and the key turn in the lock. Without a sound, the doorkeeper went by her. She beckoned. Katharina followed, her head bowed, and climbed up a narrow wooden staircase.

---

"Bless me, Reverend Father, for I have sinned." Katharina pressed her knees on the hard bench and hid her head in her hands.

"Speak, my daughter! Have you prayed ardently?"

"I believe that I have prayed poorly, too quickly and without sufficient thought."

"Why? Do you not know that Abbot Balthasar forcefully criticized you because you are so slack in your praying and singing? Your prayer is a stench instead of an offering of praise to the Highest. Why do you not pray slowly and in a strict rhythm as the rule prescribes?"

"I am always so hungry, Father."

"Hungry? You should satisfy the hunger of your soul! What is the hunger of the body by comparison? And it is not even Lent. You shall pray an additional ten *Te Deums* and tomorrow you will fast the entire day!"

"Yes, Reverend Father," Katharina said trembling.

"What else do you have to say? Investigate your conscience! Have you had unchaste thoughts?"

"I do not know what that is, Father," stammered Katharina.

"Innocent child," muttered the priest and looked with a sigh to heaven.

"God keep you in your innocence. Continue!"

"I have spoken unnecessarily."

"Why can't you women hold your tongue? How right our Father Bernard was in not wanting to put any women under his rule. With whom did you speak unnecessarily?"

"With ... with Elsa. In the cloister."

"So you will not speak to her at all for one week. I have heard that your friendship has already become an offence to others. The brides of Christ are all alike in beauty and honour before the Lord. So you should also not discriminate. You are all sisters."

"But Elsa was so severely punished. She had to clean the latrines simply because she came late to Noon Prayer and she had to ..."

"Do you presume to contradict me? Do you not know that you are obliged to be obedient, as also your sister Elsa is obliged. Remember the word of the Psalmist: 'thy loving correction shall make me great!' In this way, your sister Elsa is being made great. – What more do you have to say?"

Katharina's knees hurt. Tears fell on her hands. Her face burned. "I don't know anything more, Reverend Father."

"So, do not forget: Be quiet and pray! *Misereatur tui omnipotens deus* ... The Almighty God have mercy on you; pardon and deliver you from all your sins and lead you to everlasting life. Amen."

Katharina stood up. Barefoot, she made her way over the cold stones out of the confessional chapel and into the choir of the church. She did not dare to lift her gaze from the floor to the light coming through the windows between the narrow pillars or even to the cross under which Mary stood and stretched out her arms. All this beauty was reserved for pure souls; but she had sinned.

Ave's sister Margaret came toward here without looking up and hurried with her head bowed into the confessional booth. Katharina walked out through the small door at the north wall into the cloister. The air of the summer evening was sweet smelling and heavy. Katharina adjusted her clothing as was fitting for a nun and pulled her hands into the wide sleeves of her garment. She took a deep breath. Then she took pains to walk sedately and slowly as Sister Adelheid had taught her. And she began to pray over the great canticle of praise : *Te Deum laudamus, Te Dominum confidemur ...* We praise thee, O God, we acknowledge thee to be the Lord ...

The branches of a rose bush which blossomed in the inner court of the cloister climbed up along two pillars. Katharina stood still. A bud had opened. She spread the protecting petals far apart and laid the inside bare. Quickly a bee came and crawled in. A quiet buzzing filled the silence. *Te Aeternum Patrem omnis terra veneratur ...* All the earth doth worship thee, the Father everlasting ...

Unnoticed, another white figure appeared at her side. Aunt Lena! Magdalena von Bora laid her finger on her lips and slowly waved to Katharina to come into the inner garden of the convent which was enclosed by a high wall. Only one small gate led into it. It was secured by a large iron padlock. In the open air, Magdalena began to speak softly. "I have asked the Reverend Mother to allow you to give me a hand in the herb garden." Katharina leaped up and hugged the nun with both arms. "Slow down, my child, slow down!" Magdalena released herself gently from her clasp. She smiled. "Then, if we need more help, we will also ask for Elsa." "Oh, Aunt Lena!" "I am Sister Magdalena to you, my child." "Yes, yes, anything you say. But show me the herbs! Explain them to me!"

In the light of the warm afternoon sun, the two white forms moved back and forth between the patches. Magdalena bent down over the blossoms here and there, showing the girl the petals and the stalks. "Naturally, you know parsley. This one is absinthe, a herb for the digestion also called wormwood. It does not like to grow in the moist lowlands but we need it. You can recognize it by its tall, upright stalks and its many small leaves set in clusters of three."

A bell called them to Vespers. Magdalena and Katharina left the garden, washed their hands and faces and walked in silence with the other nuns into the tall choir of the church. Elsa joined them; she looked pale and her eyes were red from crying. Katharina's lips quivered when she saw her friend. She could hardly hold back the words she wanted to speak. She took her hand out of her sleeve instead and in the process lightly brushed Elsa's arm. A brief look ... *I am not about to confess this,* thought Katharina.

---

The summer passed. From the shadow of the cloister, Katharina occasionally looked up to the sky at the migratory flocks of birds flying south. She heard muffled sounds of harvest wagons rolling across the courtyard behind the walls. The sound of hired labourers, calling and swearing as they brought in the produce, broke the silence of her prayers.

Finally, the cattle in the pasture at the mouth of the river were driven into the sheds. Fog rose from the meadows and spread over the wide valley. It swallowed up the sound of the bells. In the courtyard, everything was empty and quiet. In the dormitory, the nuns shivered on their straw mattresses. There was deep darkness as they sang Morning Prayer and it was night again as the day closed with Compline. *Nunc dimittis servus tuum, domine, secundum verbum tuum in pace ...* (Lord, now lettest thou thy servant depart in peace, according to thy word).

Lent began and the novices were preparing for their eternal vows. Again and again with trembling lips they answered "Yes" to the question: Will you consecrate your lives to the heavenly Bridegroom and will you serve Him in obedience, chastity and poverty until He leads you into His eternal glory? They answered: "Yes!" — even though they were weak from fasting and nocturnal praying. They dragged themselves through each new day as they faced more and more new tests. Occasionally they did look at each other or Katharina would stroke Elsa tenderly on her arm as they passed one another. As they had been ordered, they did not speak to each other but they still cared for one another.

By the time spring came and at long last after all the fasting and silence, the Halleluias sounded forth again in the church, Katharina had become pale and thin. Her cheekbones protruded from her face. Her eyes burned. Again and again she was asked. Again and again she gave the answer that the rule directed,

"Yes, I do." But she hardly knew anymore what she was saying. In her dreams she saw herself standing at the door of heaven surrounded by heavenly singing.

In the autumn, the Reverend Mother felt that, after Margaret and Ave von Schoenfeld had taken their vows, Katharina should also do the same. With prayer and fasting she prepared herself for the great day. All the bells were ringing. Beams of sun streamed in through the east choir of the church. "Receive me, O Lord, and I shall live; and I shall not be confounded in my hope" As the fellowship of sisters intoned the *Te Deum*, Katharina got up from the cold stone floor. She felt the unfamiliar pressure of the veil on her shaved head. She felt faint.

But she knew what she had to do and stepped forward without hesitation so that she could throw herself on the floor in front of the chair of the abbess: *Tibi omnes angeli, tibi caeli et universae potestates ...* To thee all angels cry aloud, the heavens and all the powers therein. Margaret von Haubitz bent over and gently lifted up the prostrate girl. As Katharina looked into her face she recognized in it the expression of pain and love which had comforted her once before. *Tibi cherubim et seraphim incessabili voce proclamant: Sanctus, sanctus, sanctus dominus deus sabaoth.*

Reeling, she stood up and threw herself down in front of the prioress. Her grasp was rough, her face without expression. Next to the prioress sat Elisabeth, the oldest of the nuns. Her hands shook and her arms were without strength. "... To thee Cherubim and Seraphim continually do cry: Holy, holy, holy! Lord God of Sabaoth." Katharina staggered on, from one sister to the next. The Great *Te Deum* died away in the church. The cantor sounded the beginning of a Psalm. Katharina allowed herself to be raised up and collapsed again on the stone floor. The last nun before whom she threw herself down was Ave von Schoenfeld. She felt the gentle pressure of her hands and heard a soft murmur from Ave's mouth. Finally she was allowed to take her place in the choir. Finally she was one of them. And the nuns began another song of praise.

*This is my wedding day,* thought Katharina. She tried to sing along with the choir of the sisters but had trouble doing so. Practically unconscious from exhaustion, the tall choir of the church extended itself before her soul for a moment up to heaven. But then the singing came to an end. The abbess spoke the blessing. Magdalena came to Katharina and supported her. In silence the sisters went into the dining room. A feast was ordered. There was wild game and cake. Katharina ate only a piece of bread and a little soup. Smiling, the Reverend Mother passed her a cup of wine.

Thankful for the hour of rest after the meal, Katharina sank down on her bed. She wanted to be alone with her heavenly Bridegroom to whom she entrusted herself in a silent prayer. But instead of the great joy which she expected, she felt an inexplicable sadness in her heart. *I will never be good enough for you, my Lord Christ,* she whispered. Then she fell briefly into a deep sleep.

---

Rain fell on the stones between the pillars of the cloister. The rain drops burst and ran in all directions. A rustling and roaring filled the normally silent square between the three vaulted passage ways and the west wall of the convent building. Beneath the vaulted ceiling, it was calm. The bodies of animals looped into each other as the capitals of the columns seemed to hold their breath – at least as long as Katharina contemplated them.

She was tired as she came out of the kitchen where she had the task that week of supervising the work of the maids. There had been noise and strong smells. The copper kettles made a clanging noise. On the floor were puddles of blood and lard. On the hearth cabbage steamed. Here in the cloister, it was quiet. Suddenly she felt weary, exhausted from lack of sleep and hours of prayer. She leaned for a moment against the wall of the church which formed the border of the cloister on the north. None of the sisters were around. There was also no sound from the courtyard. The servants had crept away into the sheds and barns. The cattle were still in the fields. Like a thick blanket, the rain with its steady murmuring shut out the other noises.

Katharina's eyes followed the length of the vaulted ceilings which were attached to each other and formed a chain of arches without beginning or end. She felt the cold stone on her back and was thankful for its firmness. Somewhere a door banged. She collected herself and stood up. Two sisters came down the length of the passage. They walked slowly with bowed heads and straight backs. Katharina stepped to the side to let them pass but Magdalena von Bora looked at her and signalled with the movement of her head for her to follow them.

Now sisters also came from the other side and joined them. Several murmured a prayer. One after the other, they climbed the narrow steps to the warm room above. There was no fire burning in the hearth yet. Gertrud lay – carefully laid out – in the middle of the room. Father Boniface stood beside her, a container of consecrated oil in his hand. Silently, Katharina pressed into the corner of the room. More and more nuns came until it became crowded.

The Domina held the hand of the dying sister, Father Boniface murmured his prayer and then said to the nun in a loud voice:

"Do you acknowledge your sins? Do you acknowledge that you have not lived as your Creator wanted you to live?"

Hardly audible, the dying nun breathed her "Yes."

"Are you heartily sorry for your sins?"

"Yes."

"Are you prepared to change your ways, if God restores you to life?"

"Yes."

"Repeat after me..." In the breathless quiet, interrupted by many pauses during which Gertrud struggled for air and strength, she spoke her last prayer. "If any person has done me wrong, Lord, or if I have wronged any person, whether I have been in the right or the wrong, I commit all things completely into Your hands, Lord, whom I thank for my life ..." The last phrases were spoken in a barely audible rattle. The priest made the sign of the cross.

When the oldest of the nuns sighed, the Reverend Mother directed a reprimanding look toward her. Silently, without tears and without moving, the sisters sat by the dead nun until the clock called them to prayer. After Vespers, Katharina sat on her bed and stared into the darkness. There you will see colours ... colours ... She heard Gertrud's voice in her heart and swallowed her tears. Colours, she thought. The colours must be beautiful; and soft clothes; and the song of the angels.

She could no longer hold back her tears. She wished she could follow Gertrud into heaven. But she stayed in the darkness, clammy with the damp air. She sat and heard the others lie down, heard their soft breathing to the right and to the left. Outside, the rain continued to rustle and splash on the stones before soaking into the earth into which they would now lay Gertrud's body. For, man comes from earth and to earth ... *Inquietum est cor nostrum donec requiescat in te ...* Our heart is restless until it finds its rest in you ... She prayed for a long time in the darkness.

---

"Katharina, get up!" Elsa whispered, tugging at Katharina's limp arm.

"I am so tired."

"It is morning! The bell is calling. Do you want to sleep at the hour when our Lord rose from the dead?"

Katharina groaned. She shivered from the cold. With great difficulty, she sat up and let Elsa put her veil around her. It was still the dead of night. The stars twinkled in the wintery sky through the windows. Katharina supported herself on the arm of her friend. Silently, she joined the procession of nuns who were hurrying along in the darkness. They climbed down the steps and entered the choir loft of the church through a door held open by an unseen hand. Today they were the last ones. Every seat was already taken. Groping, Katharina found her place. She did not recognize anyone beside her but felt the breathing and shivering of the sisters. One coughed in her shawl. Another attempted silently to wipe her nose. *A solis ortu usque ad occasum:* from the rising up of the sun unto the going down of the same.

The thin voices echoed in the empty vaulted room. Katharina began to feel feverish. The words became confused in her head. She reached out, seeking help. Someone held her hot hand. Instead of singing, she could only murmur an Amen and then sank back into her chair. After the blessing, Ave and Elsa had to support her so that she could reach her bed. She didn't want to eat. In the afternoon, the Reverend Mother had her brought into the heated room. Magdalena stayed at her side.

Delirious from high fever, Katharina began to speak. She called for the small dog with which she once played in the farmhouse in Lippendorf. But no one knew what she meant. Then she spoke with her mother who was suddenly standing in front of her, very young and healthy. And at the height of the crisis, she suddenly said quite clearly and perceptibly, "Mother Mary, see my children, see my many children." When the abbess was told what Katharina had said during her fever, she shook her head in worry.

Finally, a week later, the fever abated and Katharina sat up. In the hearth a fire crackled. Through the window she saw deep snow on the roofs. She sank back with a sigh. Her garden also lay buried under the blanket of snow. Why should she get up?

Later, she heard the sisters go to prayer. There was a twitching in her arms and legs. Left alone in the gathering darkness of the room, she moved her lips and prayed with them. Then she fell asleep. Magdalena brought her some aromatic wine. "Drink, in order to regain your strength!" "Oh, Aunt Lena ..." And the nun did not refuse her familiarity. She even permitted Katharina to lay her head for a short time in her lap and close her eyes. "I would like to have gone with Gertrud to heaven."

"God grants each person her portion of time on earth," answered Magdalena. "That applies to you too."

"Yes," said Katharina obediently and sighed. "Just wait until the snow has melted again and we can go into the garden."

Magdalena smiled and nodded. "But now you must sleep. In a couple of days, you may be able to get up again. "

Katharina closed her eyes. Her aunt's voice reached her ears from a distance. She saw herself going down into the garden through the snow. The snow flakes danced in front of her face like white stars. She heard a fine high-pitched singing. And suddenly she saw a tall form clothed in a brown habit in front of her on the road. With bare feet, the man walked through the snow. This could only be St. Francis[13] about whom Sister Veronica read aloud a while ago. He went through the winter forest and, from the opposite direction, St. Clara[14] drew near, weeping and complaining. "Are you sure that we must separate? But why, my brother?"

"Do you not hear how the people speak about us? Should this holy robe become the object of ridicule? Do you not know what they are saying?"

"They do us an injustice and God is our witness," replied Clara stretching her arms toward heaven.

But the saint, who was normally so gentle, shook his head vehemently. "They are looking for reasons to ridicule me. They do not want to listen to my sermons. Any pretext will do. I want to show them that they are wrong. We must separate, my sister."

Weeping the nun turned away. "And when will I see you again, my brother?"

"When we find roses in bloom, that's when ..." They separated. The flakes of snow fell between them as a veil ... Then a cry of joy pierced the silence and St. Clara came back. Her feet flew over the white snow-covered road. She called out to him from a distance, "My brother! My brother!" Her arms were full of roses. Katharina sat upright. It was dark and quiet. There was no noise in the courtyard. The snow covered everything.

On Sunday, Katharina laboriously followed the sisters into the church. Her face was still pale, her eyes red. With a soft voice, she sang the Psalms.

"Our task is to praise our heavenly Bridegroom. There is nothing higher or more beautiful that we women can give Him," said the Reverend Mother as the sisters sat with each other after the evening meal. She scutinized the faces of the women entrusted to her. They were bent over their needlework or staring at the flickering tallow candles. Only Katharina looked intently into the eyes of the Domina. Her lips twitched but how could she ask or even contradict her? In their writings and in the stories of the saints, it was completely and uncontroversially certain that God wanted this from her, only this: chastity and poverty and obedience – obedience – obedience. Neverthe- less St. Clara found roses, roses *in the snow.*

Katharina picked up the material which she was supposed to embroider with a golden thread. She moved closer to the light. The thread glistened in her hands. She embroidered a tiny cross in the pattern on the coat. Any one of the great lords, perhaps even the Bishop of Meissen, could some day wear this garment and walk with it in front of the altar and glisten in front of the Lord with all these tiny crosses which she was embroidering – and no one would know, no one, that her fingers were sore and that her eyes burned from the smoke. So many crosses were necessary for a pattern to emerge. She stared at her hands and began a new one.

———————

The sound of calling and singing was audible in the garden. The laughter increased and died away again. A timid fiddle grated. Amidst it all, horses neighed, a drum sounded, wagons rattled by on the other side of the high wall. The three young nuns, weeding in the garden between the herbs, looked silently at one another. Finally, Elsa sat down on a stone and folded her soiled hands in her lap.

She bowed her head. "I would like to celebrate with them some time," whispered Ave.

"You are not allowed to say that."

"But what if I think it?"

Behind them they heard a rustling. Startled, Elsa looked around her. Katharina laughed. "No need to be afraid – that was only a wren."

At that very instant, the noise outside grew to a tumult. Whistling and yelling were mixed with clapping and cries of Halleluia.

"They must now be showing a piece of garment from St Mary Magdalene ..." Katharina said softly and listened intently. The tumult decreased. Several brittle women's voices sang out. "Perhaps they are now setting out the box with the drops of blood from the Apostle Paul."

Elsa studied her hands sullenly.

"I polished the gold until late into the night and when I was finished, Sister Adelheid came in and found a tiny spot of tarnish. She told me that I was unfit to do this service."

"Well, you know her, Elsa. She is old and crabby."

"Sometimes I wish I ..."

"No, Elsa. Don't say it! Don't say it!" Shocked, Katharina looked into the face of her friend. "Remember your vow."

Silently, all three of them bent over their garden beds again. Katharina plucked out the stinging nettle from between the basil and the chives. Meanwhile, Ave sneaked over to the wall. She scratched between the field stones with her finger. Elsa shook her head. Outside they were now preparing for the dance. The surrounding villages annually celebrated their convent with a festival lasting several days to commemorate the dedication of the church (for which people were promised a liberal remission of punishment for their sins)[15]. This was now reaching its high point. The young girls were shouting with joy. The men were yelling. Ave pressed her forehead against the wall and sobbed:

"I wish I could join them – I wish I could also be there!" Her companions stared at the ground.

As she straightened up, Katharina saw a white figure coming over from the convent building. Her black veil blew in the wind. She seemed to be running. "It's Veronica," said Elsa. The sister waved them over with both arms.

"She is calling us," whispered Katharina to Ave and pulled her along.

By the time they got into the chapter hall, all of the other nuns had already gathered. It was stiflingly hot in the vault. Dust was blowing in. From under their headbands sweat was running down the faces of the sisters. Katharina hid her soiled hands in her sleeves. Perplexed, she looked around. A frightening tension filled the room. With set lips, the prioress stood beside the Reverend Mother. The Domina pressed her hands together, looking uneasily from one to the other.

"Sisters, my daughters, I have called you together ... it is terrible!" Anxious murmuring erupted among the nuns. "They have pelted the vessel containing the hair of the holy Virgin Mary with stones and dirt! There are traitors among the masses who deny respect to the Mother of God. What the Evil One[16] has sown is springing up!"

"Bring the treasures back to the church!"

"Where are the guards and the hired men?"

"The Duke must send us soldiers."

"Danger! Danger!"

While several of the sisters held tightly on to their clothes as though they feared they would be robbed, others stood like statues. Margaret von Haubitz was the first to collect herself. Supported by the arm of the prioress, she raised her right hand and asked for silence.

"My daughters, whatever comes, we want to hold fast to patience and faith. I have ordered the hired men to bring all of the holy relics back into the church, to lock them up and to guard them. We must now go and have Vespers together. Has our Father Bernard not commanded us to put up prayer and silence against the noise and unrest of the world?"

The sisters bowed their heads. Katharina glanced over at Ave. She also looked uncomfortably at the floor. The young nuns prayed with ardour on this evening for grace for a world which had become disjointed and for their own sinful souls. *Domini est terra et plenitudo eius orbis terrarum et universi qui habitant in eo ...* (The earth is the Lord's and all that therein is; the compass of the world and all that dwell therein ...)

---

The festival of the dedication of the church was over. The nuns had returned their treasures to a double-locked room. On the street along the hollow, peace and quiet reigned again. Then a cold east wind came up. It whistled through the windows and drove the smoke vapours out of the chimney into the grey sky. The sisters pulled their thin coats more closely around themselves and fled into the houses. Indoors some of the warmth of summer remained, some of it also trapped within the thick walls of the church.

Katharina sat in her place in the choir loft, a book in her lap. Her black veil fell over her shoulders. Her hands moved restlessly up and down the edge of the pages. Since the sky was grey with heavy clouds, only a little light came through the window. The eternal light flickered on the altar, creating shadows in the corners. Katharina saw and heard nothing. She moved her lips as she read. Sometimes she was held up. Apparently this was not one of those passages which she had prayed a hundred times before:

> It does not help the soul if the body is adorned with the sacred robes of priests or dwells in sacred places or is occupied with sacred duties or prays, fasts, abstains from certain kinds of food or does any work that can be done by the body and in the body.

The righteousness and the freedom of the
soul requires something far different ... [17]

With a loud sigh, Katharina closed the book. The
marker at the place where she had been reading was,
however, visible between the pages. *He must be mad.
Totally delusional. Only a madman would write
something like this.* Her glance moved past the pillars
along the length of the dark wall. In the recess, in
front of which two candles burned, hung the old Pietà
canvas. With a shudder, Katharina contemplated the
battered body of the Son of God. Not only were His
hands and feet pierced; his ribs protruded from His
thin body, in His side was a terrible gaping wound and
His face was distorted in pain. One hand hung
impotent and the other was raised up, cramped in a
death grasp and yet opened as if someone should place
something into it.

The face of Mary appeared petrified from
immeasurable suffering as she held the body of her
son in both arms. It appeared as if He would slip away
from her, so light did the emaciated body seem to be.
*Oh Mother of Sorrows,* sighed Katharina. *It is good that I
don't have any sons. I could not bear it.* Bearly audible, a
door creaked. Katharina held her breath. She pressed
the book tightly to herself. Two sisters crept into the
choir loft. One of them sat beside her. Katharina
exhaled and opened the book again.

"Ave, it is so terrible to read this. Where did you get
this book?"

"Psst!" The second nun, Ave's sister, furtively
looked around. "Give it back to us if you don't want to
read it any more"

Katharina shook her head vehemently. "No. No.
Leave it with me until tomorrow. I will then exchange
my prayerbook with you and you will find the sheets in
it."

They became quiet. Katharina tried to decipher the next section in the dim light.

> The things which have been mentioned could be done by any wicked person. Such works produce nothing but hypocrites ... On the other hand, it will not harm the soul if the body is clothed in secular dress, dwells in unconsecrated places, eats and drinks as others do, does not pray aloud, and neglects to do all the above-mentioned things.

"Was everything then for nought, Eva?" whispered Katharina to the sister. "All the praying and fasting and singing of Psalms?"

"Precisely. It was for nought," answered Ave softly and with a firm voice. "But – this is just one person saying so! Only one against all the others, our Father Bernard, St. Benedict, the Pope, the bishops ..."

"Nevertheless."

The door opened again. This time it was the sexton who came in to light the candles on the altar and to ring the bells. Katharina closed the book. More and more of the other sisters slipped in. Chairs creaked. One heard soft sighs and prayers. As the bells ceased, the cantor began Vespers. Katharina opened her mouth to sing along: " *Ecce ancilla domini* ..." Behold, the handmaiden of Lord – but her heart fluttered like a bird under her white garment.

After the evening meal which the sisters customarily ate in silence, the abbess called the convent together in the chapter hall. The Domina was restless. With the long small hand on which her ring glistened, she fingered and pulled her garment into proper place. Silently the sisters waited until everyone had found her place. Then the Reverend Mother began to speak.

"A report has come from our town of Grimma ..." Katharina hardly dared to breath. She glanced at the faces of the other sisters who looked at the Domina with great attentiveness. "The convent of the Augustinian-Eremites [18] has ... has disbanded itself."

Shocked, the nuns winced. Those who sat in the front turned around and directed their gaze at those in the back rows. In their midst sat two nuns who had to know more, the sisters Zeschau. Did not their uncle, the prior of this fellowship, visit them a few days earlier — in monk's garb, as a pious, holy man?[19] Would one have permitted him to come into the visitors' room, had it been known that he came from the deserters who followed the deceiver, their brother from the Augustinian order at Wittenberg? The Zeschau sisters sat motionless. In the midst of the agitation, they appeared to be the only ones who knew what they had to do. The one humbly kept her head bowed. The other looked thoughtfully at the cross which was fastened to the wall above the abbess.

"The teachings of the apostate monk from Wittenberg have now also reached our region," the Domina continued. "We must now build a protective wall, not around our convent – its walls are high enough – but around our hearts. If one of you ever comes into possession of the damnable tracts with which this servant of the Devil poisons pious souls, you are duty-bound to hand them over to me! Immediately! And without reading them. I will not read them either but will hand them over to the purifying flames, lest our bodies burn in eternity."

She dropped her voice and lifted both hands imploringly: "Sisters, remember your vows. You do not belong to yourselves. Do not allow yourselves to be misled!"

Katharina thought she felt the eyes of the Reverend Mother on her bowed head. And yet, she was not the only one! Under her veil, she glanced to the side and tried to see where Elsa was sitting. Her friend sat on a bench by the window and appeared to look with disinterest out of the window.

There was a sudden commotion in the back corner. Old Elisabeth had jumped up, waved her arms and stepped panting forward: "I saw a beast rising out of the sea with ten horns and seven heads." She became incoherent and her voice broke off. Her entire body shook. Two of the sisters had to hold her.

"Amen, Amen," others in the room called out. An uneasy quiet spread throughout the room.

That night, Katharina lay awake in her bed and listened. Were not the others also breathing uneasily? Was that not a sigh she heard? Were not other sisters tossing uneasily back and forth as she was? From the forest, an owl hooted. Katharina sank into the darkness. Suddenly a great iron gate opened. A jet of fire shot out. She wanted to escape but there was no road, no path. From every side, monsters like giant insects flew at her. They seized her to toss her into a huge fire in which arms and legs jerked and long hair waved.

"Quiet, Katharina." She awoke bathed with sweat. Elsa sat at her side.

"I ... I was in hell."

Her friend hurried quietly back to her bed. Katharina tried to pray: *Omnipotens sempiterne deus* ... Almighty and everlasting God, in whose hands dwell all might and the rights of every people: ... But her head throbbed. Every throb was a word and the words formed a sentence. It was always the same: "A Christian ... is a perfectly free lord of all ... of all ... of all ... " Suppose this monk is right, suppose he is right![20]

---

Deep in thought, Katharina walked to and fro in the cloister. Her lips moved mechanically and murmured prayers so that none of the sisters, not even the strict prioress or suspicious old Elisabeth could have seen anything bar a pious, God-fearing nun. But Katharina's thoughts jumped over the wall of the convent, wandered across the wide expanse of the fields where the first green plants had appeared, followed the horsemen who galloped down the street with sealed letters in their pockets, and tried to awaken out of her memory the feel of a swinging coach.

She gave a sudden start. A heavy hand was on her shoulder. She turned her head. Behind her stood Magdalena von Staupitz,[21] a dignified, tall woman with a small face.

"You have also written a letter?" she asked in a whisper.

"Yes," said Katharina. The older woman looked her in the eyes suspiciously.

"Do you know what you are doing?"

"I know," Katharina answered defiantly.

Sister Magdalena let her arm sink and her hand disappeared again into her broad sleeve.

"To whom did you write?"

"To my oldest brother, Hans von Bora."

"Do you think he will take you in?" Katharina could stand the stern look no longer. She pressed her lips together and looked at the floor.

"I don't know," she answered hesitatingly. In her mind was a picture of a grinning boy chasing his dog towards the chickens.

"None of us know," sighed the other. "But I fear that no one out there will want us – except, perhaps, one; the one with whom it all began, whose thoughts burn within us as fire."

"Do you believe that the monk himself ... Do you believe that he will help us?"

Magdalena shrugged her shoulder. Her face showed helplessness and worry. More gently, she looked down at Katharina:

"I should not have given you the tract. I bear the responsibility. I am the oldest. But perhaps you will have it easier because you are still young. If it succeeds, if ..."

She turned to go. She took a couple of steps, then turned and whispered:

"Tomorrow, merchant Koppe out of Torgau is coming to bring fresh goods. I heard Domina speak of it. Perhaps he will also bring letters. Be ready – after Vespers, in the pharmacy."

Magdalena walked away with hurried steps. She went through the small door into the church. Feeling lost and helpless, Katharina remained behind. Would anyone want her? Hans is married, perhaps he has children already. Children!

She swallowed violently. She could work anywhere; in the barn; in the kitchen; with the children; in the garden. She pulled her hands out of her white sleeves and studied them: hands for doing things, hands for working; hands for stroking, yes, for stroking ... Suddenly tears fell on them. With loud sobbing, Katharina grasped the column in front of her and pressed her hot forehead against it. The stone was cold and dead.

———————

Since the garden of the convent was in full bloom in May, Katharina went out after Vespers to pick a bouquet which she wanted to bring to the canvas of the Mother of Sorrows. She gathered up her wide white garment and was careful not to step on a snail or kill a beetle. She took some of the lilies which had just begun to bloom and searched for a red blossom to place into the cluster of white blossoms like the bleeding heart of the Mother of God. Just then she saw Elsa coming. Her friend walked slowly. As she came closer, Katharina knew that something was wrong.

"Elsa, what is it? What has happened?"

"I have received an answer – from my sister."

"Just as all of us," said Katharina bitterly and put her arm around Elsa's shoulders. They hugged each other and stood without a word. The flowers which Katharina was carrying fell to the ground.

"They don't want us. That's the only reason why they entrusted us to the heavenly Bridegroom. The monk is right. It is hypocrisy. They do it as if they want to serve God ..."

"God has forgotten us, Katharina. We are forgotten brides – while the entire world prepares for the wedding feast."

"No, Elsa, no. We will also be there. We will!" They released each other and while Katharina gathered up her flowers, Elsa counted all of the sisters who had asked their relatives to take them out of the convent.

"Only three – only three out of twelve would be taken up in love if they left the convent. And we, we must remain. But Magdalena said, if our relatives won't help us, then we should ask him. Luther? Yes, the monk, the heretic, the prophet, the one who knows so much about us and the anxiety of our souls; the one who knows so much about fasting and praying and how little it benefits. Are you listening? All of us, whom no one wants, we will ask Luther for help. We will dare to do it. He has so many friends, say the sisters. He will help us. He has to do it, he has to do it."

The two young women stood still and looked up into the evening sky.

"There are no walls," whispered Elsa. "Yes, God will help us. Amen."

---

The small door in the wall was open. No one knew who had opened it. Katharina saw only shadows and heard the rustle of clothes. Nothing else could be seen or heard; no road, no path, no call. It was the darkest night of the year, the night of deepest silence – before the Easter celebration would break forth. In the evening in the church, they had snuffed out all the candles. After all, He was dead, their Lord. His body perished on the cross. His cry had died away. Katharina had snuffed out as the last light the one which burned in front of the Vesper picture and she looked once more into the face of Mary holding her martyred Son. And she knew then that if she ever had a son, she would also have to suffer. In the convent, she would have been secure ...

As the sisters went their way in silence, Katharina wandered, as if by chance, past Aunt Lena and pressed her hand. She could not see the face of Magdalena and didn't want to. Her friends tossed to and fro on their beds until they heard the call of the owl. It called as always – yet different. They were the only ones who counted: once, twice, three times – and again: once, twice, three times. Then they knew. The call was for them.

Katharina shivered. The stone wall along which she was groping was cold. In the cloister, she encountered Veronica. They pushed each other forward. Others forms hurried beside them into the garden. Magdalena von Staupitz was among them, taller than all of them. Outside, a strong hand grabbed Katharina. Someone lifted her up. She felt the wood of the wagon on her back and the warmth of the sisters beside her. Then the horses began to pull. The harnesses jangled! Will not everyone in Throne of Mary wake up?

The horses began to trot. Weakened from fatigue and fasting, the nuns faded in and out of consciousness. A pointy elbow pressed into Katharina's chest. She did not dare to move. Elsa's ice-cold hand lay on hers. They were all only one shivering body, only one beating heart. The horses soon appeared to have firm ground beneath their hooves. The road to Grimma ... Magdalena began to pray. *Pater noster, qui es in caelis ...* Our Father, who art in heaven ... The others whispered along, some louder, others softer. It seemed to Katharina that the wagon was flying. Had God sent His angel? For a short time she slept, her head leaning on Ave's shoulder. Then light glimmered through the narrow opening of the covered wagon.

*"Resurrexi et adhuc tecum sum ..."* whispered Elsa. I arose, and am still with Thee.

*"Alleluja. Posuisti super me manum tuam."* Alleluia; Thou hast laid Thy hand upon me, answered Katharina jubilantly.

"Psst," whispered Magdalena, who still feared for the safety of the fugitives.[22] But then a jovial voice from the driver's seat called,

"Don't be afraid, dear nuns. Don't be afraid anymore. The sun is rising and no one is pursuing us. The trick has worked. You are safe."

The wagon stopped. The canvas covering was thrown back. Three men legs astride, one with white hair and two younger ones, stood looking down at the women. Their round faces smiled and the eyes of the younger men flashed with satisfaction at their own daring. The sisters sat up and gently stretched their aching arms and legs. Katharina blinked at the morning light and saw the broad landscape covered with new green growth. The sun was rising over it, bright and red. The forest seemed to be in flames and yet it did not burn up. The sisters sat breathless in a huddle. With a loud voice, Magdalena began to speak the prayer from the Easter mass:

"O God, who on this day, through Thine only begotten Son has overcome death and opened to us the gate of everlasting life; do Thou follow with Thine aid the desires which Thou dost put into our minds, and by Thy continual help, bring the same to good effect. Through the same Jesus Christ." All of them prayed along.

The old merchant[23] removed his cap from his head and devoutly folded his hands. The younger men stood a bit removed and grinned. Amen, one of the two finally called and snapped his whip impatiently.

"Onward to Torgau! Soon you will see the brightly shining towers of the city." The wagon swung into motion. The nuns left the canvas covering folded back and looked out. How beautifully God's earth lay before them. They could not stop praising and thanking Him as they joyfully sang the Easter Psalm: *Haec dies quam fecit dominus ...* This is the day that the Lord has made; let us rejoice and be glad ...

# Torgau/Wittenberg 1523-1528

The bells rang as the wagon rolled through the bumpy streets of Torgau. Breathless, the nine nuns sat under the canvas cover which Herr Koppe had closed up again as the wagon drew near to the city. They heard the noise of the city and the mocking greetings being hurled at the driver.

"So Herr Leonhard, are you working even today? Can you not earn enough with your goods? Look. He has his wagon full and is heading to the castle. Will there be a feast?"

Young Koppe answered excitedly, "Yes. Yes. You sleepy heads. We have precious freight. Before you got up out of the straw, we were already celebrating resurrection!" Katharina raised the canvas a little. She didn't see much: strong legs in tight shoes; barefooted children; an old woman, so bent over that she practically crept on the ground; boots, big and heavy.

She almost fell out of the wagon for it suddenly turned sharply to the right. Ave and Margaret slipped from their places and let out a muted scream. The horses stopped. Koppe senior threw back the canvas covering. Out, he called with a friendly laugh. Here you can find initial refuge. The nuns jumped down and stood reeling in the light of day. Almost immediately, they were surrounded by such a large group of people that no one could pass in the narrow street. The children in the front looked at the unfamiliar women wide-eyed. And with exactly the same look of amazement the nuns looked back into the faces of the children.

"Truly, we must be an interesting spectacle," Magdalena finally said, "with our rumpled veils and dishevelled head-covering. Come. We are going into the house, sisters!"

Accustomed to obeying orders, the others followed her into the dark hall of the spacious house filled with the smell of a delicious roast. A friendly, plump woman met them. However, helplessness also showed on her face as she saw the nine women.

"Mother, bring them something to eat and don't stare at them as if you have never seen a bride of Christ before," called Koppe through the door to her. Then the woman impulsively grabbed Veronica who stood closest to her and hugged her.

"My, you are thin," she cried. "Did you have to fast so severely?" With a wave of her hand she sent off the speechless, amazed maids into the kitchen. Then she led the nuns up a narrow staircase into a bright attic where several straw mattresses were lying on the well-swept floor. "We do not have any more room than this but then you will not be staying long. Don't any of you have any luggage? One piece of clothing? Oh, Jesus and Mary! Where do we start? We had best begin by eating – evidently, you are not able to talk. Oh, do remove the veils from your heads! Perhaps the neighbors can find you a couple of dresses. Put your veils around your shoulders. That looks a little less holy. Oh, you all have such pointed noses. We had better put a couple more chickens into the soup. How can a person allow young people to starve themselves like this and all for the sake of heavenly salvation? But, Luther knows better ..."

Murmuring and scolding, groaning and moaning, the woman let herself down the narrow stairway again and left the nuns alone. They sat on the floor and looked helplessly at one another. From outside came the noise of scolding, beating drums, loud laughter, neighing of horses, and the cry of children. A wagon rattled by. A whip cracked. Loud steps approached and died away.

While Katharina listened anxiously, Ave walked to the dormer window through which the daylight came into the room.

"Oh, have a look."

Everyone crowded around her to catch a glimpse. Katharina stood on tiptoe and over the heads of the others caught sight of the pointed tile roofs, the chimneys and — over there were towers which rose up so high above the houses that she thought this must be the heavenly Jerusalem. How the stones glistened! And up above, the blue spring sky stretched out into the distance.

"The castle of the Elector," [24] explained Margaret. At that moment the bells began to ring anew. From many sides, the Easter jubilation made it sound as though every house in this city had a bell. The walls seemed to quake and the nuns sank to their knees. Katharina felt tears falling down her cheeks. But instead of wiping them away, she began to laugh uncontrollably. The others joined in. They grasped each other's hands and, while the bells of Torgau called the news across the land, they danced their dance of joy bent over in the low ceilinged storeroom of merchant Koppe.

Two days later, Koppe's wagon again rolled through Torgau. In the narrow streets he had to make his way laboriously between the farm wagons and riders, the gaping market women and the crying children. Koppe greeted the gatemen from his seat.

"Where are you going?"

"To Wittenberg."

Huddled close together again, the nine nuns sat behind Koppe's broad back. But they no longer had the canvas cover drawn over their heads. Lively and interested, they looked out at the world. And where the children waved, they waved joyfully back. Gradually, they left the city with its walls and towers behind. Only occasionally did they meet a person walking or in a cart. The wind whistled across the plain. In front of them lay the long, straight road.

———————————

Never, thought Katharina, had she seen so many people in one place. People were jostling, pushing and shoving one another all along the bank of the River Elbe and through the town gate.

"Make way," yelled Koppe and cracked his whip. "Don't you students ever have anything better to do? " In fact, it was mainly well-dressed young gentlemen who stood along the way, their mouths open in amazement. Behind them a couple of women with large baskets pushed forward. Between the legs of the adults pressed the children – and everyone stood there wide-eyed as if Herr Koppe had brought real angels from heaven to Wittenberg. With difficulty he navigated the wagon through the gate and turned right.

"Don't be afraid, young ladies," he called back. "These are the Wittenbergers![25] They have nothing better to do than to make funny faces. But we are almost there." And he pointed with his whip at a large house separated from the street by a yard full of large trees.

Wrrr ... The wagon veered into the yard and the horses stood still. Koppe threw the reins to his nephew and jumped from the seat. The people remained behind on the street with only a couple of curious boys following them almost to the door of the house. An expectant silence filled the air. Everyone now looked toward the entrance of the house at which Koppe knocked loudly. The door opened and the merchant disappeared inside. Katharina fiddled with her shawl, a gift from Frau Koppe to cover her bald skull. Her heart beat violently. Mixed images passed in front of her eyes, always wilder, always more quickly. Then she heard whispering all around her. In fearful expectation, she looked up. The door of the house had opened and in the shadow of the entrance stood a man. With his full black habit, he almost filled the doorway.

"Come in, young ladies," he called across the yard in a loud voice and stretched out his arms invitingly.

———————————

From Bürgemeister Alley to the house of Professor Philipp Melanchthon[26] was no farther than from the herb garden of the convent to the chapter hall. At times it seemed to Katharina that the whole of Wittenberg with its walls[27] and large market place was like a large convent. The gardens were behind the houses bordering the Elbe. Around the garden area was another outer defensive ring. And at night, the gates were tightly locked. But there was more excitement in the market place than there had been in the isolated convent while during the day, the gates were open to all travellers. Women and men hurried down the streets. Children tumbled down the lanes. Dogs dug around in the piles of rubbish. Even in the evening, the noise and clamour did not decrease very much, for when the citizens went to sleep the students began their nocturnal life. One could hear their singing until the morning hours and it became quiet about the time the bell rang in the new day.

Since her arrival, Katharina had been living in the house of the town-clerk, Reichenbach on Bürgemeister Alley. She helped his wife and was treated like their daughter. But, though she was eager to leave the house to smell, feel and hear the spring, her heart beat loudly and violently every time she walked through town. In the meadows of the Elbe River, the frogs croaked. A blackbird sang his shrill song in the lime tree. It was on an evening made for a walk that Katharina left the house with a basket full of finely embroidered laundry which Frau Reichenbach had requested her to bring to Melanchthon's house.

She was wearing a simple unpretentious dress whose material was somewhat threadbare in a number of places – for which reason Frau Reichenbach had discarded it. The bodice, however, still showed its artful embroidery and it was tied so tightly that Katharina's slender waist and full bosom were accentuated. Beneath her matching embroidered cap, her hair had also begun to grow. Every evening as she removed her stiff head covering, Katharina gently touched the soft down on her head. Each time she feared anew that her hair would not grow anymore or that it would fall out again. But right from the beginning, Frau Melanchthon had laughed and told her,

"Hair is like grass – it always keeps growing!"

With her accustomed erect posture and without showing her fear, Katharina crossed the threshold to the safety of the house. She still had the constant fear with every step that she would fall down into an abyss. She didn't know what to do with her hands; she would have preferred to hide them in her sleeves but they were cut much too narrow. She barely looked up so she almost bumped into an old man who limped towards her. The old man stopped and shook his head.

"Hey, Fräulein ..." Katharina did not have the courage to reply to him and hurried on. She still felt unable to speak to a strange man on the street. Then a small dog ran yelping between her feet and children came running from the market. Breathing heavily, she remained standing where she was.

Two elegantly dressed townswomen walked along on the other side of the street.

"Good evening, gnädiges Fräulein!" one of them called in a light mocking tone. Softly, the other one said,

"Is it not a little late for a nun to be out?" Giggling, the two went on. Katharina clutched her basket more tightly and looked after them. She pressed her lips tightly together. With angry determination, she continued on her way. As she neared the house of Melanchthon beside the university, she saw that from the other side – from the direction of the Elster Gate – someone was heading for the same destination. Her heart began to beat wildly again. It was a monk, bulky and large in his black habit, solid as a rock in the middle of the street. She looked down and stood still.

"Well, Fräulein von Bora, are we both going to visit our friend Melanchthon?"

"Please, Herr Doktor, go ahead. I ... I have something ... something to bring to Frau Melanchthon." Her stuttering upset her and she wished she had a veil in front of her face. Luther was already knocking with heavy blows on the door of the dilapidated house. As it opened, he turned to Katharina:

"Come, mein Fräulein ... Let me show you proper honour," and he bade her go in first.

She quickly followed the servant into the servants' quarters while Luther walked into the family living room. Loud voices and laughter came from the living room. There must have been four or five men gathered there but Melanchthon's wife[28] also sat at the table – and so, Fräulein von Bora was invited to join them. They greeted her in a friendly manner.

"This, dear Hieronymus,[29] is one of the nine nuns which our dear Doktor freed through his personal intervention," said the host to his neighbour.

The young man with long brown locks wore a richly adorned garment and a golden chain. With sparkling eyes, he looked at Katharina.

"You have to agree that it is a great sin of the papacy to hide such noble women from us men," declared Melanchthon's friend Camerarius[30] with a wide sweeping gesture as if he wanted to bring his accusation to the pope personally. Katharina remained silent.

"But hey, old chap, she has not yet learned frivolous banter," continued Camerarius jovially. "That is why she stands here with an aura of sanctity. The students call her Katharina of Sienna." [31]

"Sometimes people confuse pride with holiness," said Melanchthon's wife snidely. "A noble maiden doesn't speak to just anyone."

The window allowed too little daylight through for anyone to see Katharina's face turn red.

"At least I am not used to being ridiculed," she said, getting up with a start. The young stranger jumped to his feet, took her hand and bowed in front of her.

"Mein Fräulein, do not take the mocking of these men, who are normally so earnest, as an expression of dishonour to you – and be assured of this: we all bow before you with greatest respect for the courage you have shown!" He sat down again. The hostess showed Katharina to a place in the corner of the room and the evening conversation of the learned friends proceeded. However, Katharina could no longer keep her eyes off the stranger. It was as if he had opened a door to a hidden room in her heart, a room which was still shrouded in deep darkness.

---

Two days later on the way to the market, Katharina saw the attractive young man again. As he hurried toward her, she stood still, as if struck by a blow. She almost dropped her basket as he said, "Fräulein von Bora. How nice to see you again."

She cautiously raised her eyes. "I am also pleased to see you." Were her eyes sparkling too much? Fearfully, she lowered her eyes again.

"Are you going to the market?"

"Yes. Frau Reichenbach, who has accepted me as a daughter into her house, asked me to buy vegetables. I am happy to do it even if it is actually the work of the maids. They bring home cabbage which is full of maggots. They hardly recognize which fruit is ripe and which is not. In addition, they allow themselves to be cheated by the tradesmen and I count every penny. Reichenbach has been so good to me – even this dress."

"It looks very lovely on you," said Hieronymus without taking his eyes off her face. His small lips under his brown moustache smiled in friendly manner. "I notice that you are also quite capable of speaking – Saint Katharina! I believe it only needs someone to unlock your mouth."

She was too taken aback to carry on talking. Had she spoken too much? What was the source of all these words?

"Would you open up a little more if I invite you to take a walk with me by the gate this evening?" Katharina hesitated for a moment because her heart threatened to skip a beat. But then she answered quickly:

"I will ask the master for permission! Come to the door when the evening bell rings." She extended her hand to him which he warmly pressed. Then she turned quickly and plunged into the throng in the market place. She walked with upright posture and a bright look, testing out the goods, comparing prices, and did not listen to the murmuring behind her back:

"Here ... this one here. Yes, one of them ... still in Wittenberg ... Here, your ladyship, buy from me! Not from the others! ... most of them are already gone ... there were nine, yes ... all from noble families ... looking for husbands ... if they can do it ... you know what! Here are the nicest berries ... Have you tried them already, gnädiges Fräulein? Herring like in the convent ..."

---

The lime trees were in bloom. Their scent filled the evening air in the town weary of the summer heat. The students had gone in small groups to the river to refresh themselves. Their noise could be heard in the distance. Katharina sat at a window and busied herself with some embroidery. But her thoughts wandered to the gate, to the blooming borders which ran around to the birch grove. In the hall, she heard steps.

"Katharina," called the mistress of the house. Relieved, she put her work aside and stood up. The door opened and Hieronymus stormed in. Silently, Katharina looked toward him with a smile.

"I have come, my love, to say farewell to you."

"So soon?"

"The sooner I get to Nurenberg to speak to my parents, the sooner I will be back to fetch you."

He grasped her hands and looked at her lovingly. "And then Saint Katharina of Sienna will become the wife of Hieronymus Baumgaertner, who is not at all a saint." He laughed heartily. "But your parents! Do you think they will agree to it? So quickly ..." With a motion of his hands, Hieronymus waved the concern away and sat down beside Katharina at the window.

"Consider also how dangerous the way is. There is so much talk about people being beaten and robbed on the highways. Even the farmers travel in groups for protection. Would God not give me a couple of angels to accompany me? Will not my love pray for me – four times a day?"

"Nine times," said Katharina laughing. She breathed heavily. For a while they sat silently side by side. He held her hands and stroked them softly. From downstairs, one could hear the sound of pots in the kitchen and maids laughing. Otherwise it was silent in the house.

"Herr Doktor Martinus laughed happily when I told him. 'One less worry,' he said. And he has truly earned a lightening of his load of worries. He has enough other worries!" continued Hieronymus joyfully. "You will like Nurenberg! Nothing against Wittenberg but, you know, among us in Nurenberg everything is somewhat more elegant. And the countryside is not so boring, flat and sandy! The fortress towers proudly over the rooftops! And when you travel down the broad streets and see our beautiful house, well decorated and with a large alcove."

As Hieronymus related these things, Katharina looked out at the lime trees. She imagined the fortress, the street, the house. In her thoughts, she walked beside of her husband up the staircase, stepped into a bright room adorned with a carpet ... And tears flowed down her face.

"Don't cry, my Katharina."

"I am only crying because I am happy, Hieronymus," she said, embarassed. "And are you absolutely sure that you will return?"

"Yes, I promise you. Just be happy each day." As it became dark, Hieronymus bid farewell to Reichenbach and his wife and left. Katharina heard the sound of his steps on the street. She sat for a long time at the window, her needlework on her lap. She wanted to pray but the right words wouldn't come. So she clasped her hands and merely stammered beneath her tears: *Miserere mei, deus, miserere mei ...* Have mercy on me, O God, have mercy on me ...

———————

"What are you bringing to me, Katharina?" asked Reichenbach who, in spite of the summer heat, was sitting covered with a blanket in the room.

"Good sir, this is a brew of Menyanthes trifoliata, which I found for you on the river bank. It will do you good. In the convent, we ... "

"I didn't know, my dear, that you understood anything about the art of healing."

"Oh, we had an excellent pharmacy. My Aunt Magdalena worked there and taught me about the use of herbs." Involuntarily, Katharina sighed at the thought of her aunt who now had to carry on in the pharmacy by herself. "Take and drink, even if it tastes bitter. You will feel better afterward!" Reichenbach took the mug out of Katharina's hand and put it to his mouth. After the first sip, he shivered:

"That really is a bitter medicine. But to please you, I will gulp it down."

Thankful, he smiled at the young woman who bent over him with care as she adjusted his foot rest.

"May I ask you something, sir?"

"You can always do that, Katharina."

"I would like to do something useful. And here in the house there are so many maids and very little work. I ..." She became embarassed and quiet.

"So, what useful thing can you do?" asked Reichenbach somewhat amused.

"As I went out to search for herbs this afternoon, I thought ... I did enjoy it so. Could I perhaps help out in the pharmacy with Meister Lucas?[32] They also have small children. I know from my sister Ave how much work there is to do there."

"If you were to give everyone who comes into the pharmacy such a bitter drink," said Reichenbach smiling, "Meister Lucas would soon be without customers! However, I will speak to him as soon as your infusion has helped me. My wife has also said that you have no great inclination for domestic work like embroidery and sewing. Our daughters always filled the time before their weddings in this way. But why should you not help instead at Cranachs? You will find a large household there and you can certainly learn a great deal. Only, don't become infected by the vanity of the house-mistress."

Feeling tired, he leaned back in his armchair and studied Katharina who had remained standing in front of him.

"You have conducted yourself quietly and well with us, Katharina, but I have noticed that our house is too small for you."

"Oh, no – it is only that I am not suited for some of the work. My fingers are so clumsy when I hold a needle."

"I will see what can be done."

Quietly, Katharina went out of the room and crept down the stairs. Oh, if only she were not so impatient! Eight long weeks had already passed since Hieronymus had taken his leave. And each day, each hour she waited, standing by the window, wandering restlessly through the quiet rooms, going out on to the street, looking into the face of every stranger. But there was no message from him. Would he come soon himself? Perhaps tomorrow? Or the next day? After allowing the noonday heat to pass, Katharina took a walk across the market place to the street which led to the castle (the pharmacy was located at that end of the market place). Well acquainted with the surroundings, Katharina crept across the yard through the small door that led into the house. In the back room of the pharmacy between the carefully ordered bottles and glasses, she found the young medical doctor, Doktor Basilius – and Ave standing beside him with radiant eyes.

Startled, Katharina asked, "Am I intruding?"

"No, you're not!" answered Ave laughing as she hugged her convent sister. The young doctor gave a friendly smile.

"You both look as though you're celebrating." Ave blushed but remained quiet. Katharina would have liked to rejoice with them. But a painful feeling of abandonment suddenly possessed her and she turned away. Through the front door came the mistress of the house, behind her a trader whom she had brought with her from the street.

"Come, Katharina," she called enthusiastically. "Come into my room. Let's check out the fabrics this man imported from Italy. You have never seen anything this wonderful." Talking cheerfully, Barbara Cranach climbed up the stairs and Katharina had no choice but to follow her. After she had studied the fine fabrics, Barbara finally asked: "And how is it going with your good Meister? Has his stomach settled down yet?"

"I very much hope so," said Katharina and laughing related the account of the bitter infusion which she had prepared for him — and about her wish to work in the pharmacy.

"Until Hieronymus returns," said Barbara. Katharina swallowed. "What feasts we will have in our house! First, we will marry off Ave to Doktor Basilius and then you with Hieronymus. How pleased I am; but what is wrong with you, Katharina? Why are you not happy?"

"I will only be happy when ... when Hieronymus is here."

"He will come soon; be absolutely sure of it." Barbara took a width of the finest, light-brown cloth and laid it over Katharina's shoulder. Then she took one of the thick gold chains from her neck and hung it for effect around the neck of the young woman. "You will be beautiful, Katharina, beautiful and proud as a patrician! Then she clapped her hands cheerfully: "But first I have to teach you how to preside over a large household!"

---

In Cranach's house, the days seemed to pass more quickly than at Reichenbach's. Early in the morning the apprentice painters streamed noisily into the workplace and began their work under the guidance of the Meister and his son, Hans. During that time, Ave and Katharina took care of the younger children of the family and the mistress of the house busied herself with the buying and the allocation of duties in the kitchen. If there was a lot to do in the pharmacy, Ave helped with the sales while Katharina helped with enthusiasm in the preparation of mixtures and salves. Attentively, she often listened to what was happening in the studio. However, the women seldom saw the pictures which came into being there. One evening, however, as the Meister worked alone, they asked if he would let them into the studio.

"This, Fräulein von Bora, is a portrait of our late Elector,[33] whom we can thank that we can follow the new teaching in freedom and peace! I am just at the point of 'dressing up' his fur coat," explained Cranach. The grim face of the Elector made Katharina afraid but she also noticed that his eyes looked friendly and quiet. And she knew: this man held his protecting hand over her as she fled the convent and as the Reverend Mother had come with the Abbot of Pforta and bitterly complained ... While the painter worked by the final light of the day with the paint brush on the fur collar of the Elector, Katharina walked devoutly from one easel to another.

"Do not be shocked, Fräulein von Bora," said Cranach with a sideways look as he saw that she drew near to a wooden easel with a prostrate water nymph far back in the corner and half covered with a cloth. But it was too late.

"Who – who is this, Meister Lucas?"

"A nymph, my child. The Greeks believed that springs, brooks and rivers contained spirits which looked like beautiful women."

Relieved, Katharina regained her breath. "So – it is not an actual woman?"

"No, my dear bride of Christ," said Cranach with a mischievous laugh. "Not an actual woman. But such beautiful women do exist." Katharina did not dare to ask any more but walked to the next picture. There she saw a richly clothed young lady under a tall tree. In her hands, she held a vessel. Her face was very graceful and beautiful but very serious.

"That is St Magdalena with her jar of ointment. Do you believe, Meister Lucas, that she was this beautiful?"

"Of course. She was, after all, a great sinner." This answer also greatly amazed Katharina. She looked carefully at the face of the saint.

"I believe we can call it a day," said Cranach and laid aside his paintbrush. He wiped his hands on a towel and cast one more critical eye on his work. He turned to go and Katharina followed him. As they were going out, she turned around once more and looked at the white body of the prostrate naked nymph glowing in the half-darkness of the studio.

---

One noon at the family table, Meister Lucas winked over at Ave and Katharina.

"We already have two young noble women in the family – and now a real king will come to visit." Pleased, he stroked his pointed beard. "What an important place our Wittenberg is!"

"A king?" Little Lucas looked questioningly at his father. "Does he wear a golden crown?" chimed inhis sister.

"I am afraid that he has lost his golden crown on the way," Meister Lucas said laughing. "He is as poor as a church mouse and will be thankful to be allowed to sit at Frau Barbara's table."

Later that same evening, there was a loud knocking at the gate. The servants ran with torches to open it wide. Meister Lucas walked into the hall wearing a big black coat. Barbara stood beside him adorned in a splendid collar. Ave and Katharina stood with the children behind the master of the house and his wife. From outside, where it was raining heavily, came a strong young man in dark clothes. His face was pale, his eyes furtive. Two servants led the horses. Luther, broad and quiet, was the last one to enter the house. Water was running down his black locks into his face.

"Welcome, King Christian,[34] into the house of a simple townsman," said Cranach and turning to Luther he added, "Come in, Herr Doktor, before you get entirely soaked." Luther laughed.

"You are right. I should bring my new garment which the goodness of the Elector has bestowed on me out of the rain!"

"Indeed, Doktor," called Barbara, disregarding the noble guest. "You have removed the monk's habit. It is about time!"

"He to whom kings turn for help also has the right to a decent garment," growled Cranach and invited the guests into the living room. A fire burned in the hearth. The windows were locked with wooden shutters so that a cosy warmth quickly spread out causing steam to rise from the wet clothes of the guests.

Christian II of Denmark walked restlessly back and forth at the side of the room as the friends spoke. The children stared at him fearfully until Ave took them up to their bedroom. Katharina stayed behind with the Cranachs. The maid placed a light on the table and filled the silver beaker.

"Come, your Majesty. Even though they have driven you out of your country, let us drink to the spread of the good Lutheran teaching in Denmark!" The king grabbed the beaker and drank hastily. Then he turned to the women and, without saying a word, lifted the beaker again. Katharina looked into his tired face, encircled by a dark beard. She felt sympathy for the stranger but as they went up the stairs after the meal, Barbara whispered to her:

"Did you see his hands? They are so white and soft, yet they have blood on them. Lucas said that he had a great number of the Swedish nobility killed." [35]

The next day was clear and beautiful. The autumn sun shone over little Wittenberg. While King Christian and a member of the elector's council, who had come by from Torgau, spoke about the situation in the northern countries, Katharina went to the bank of the Elbe to gather herbs. The river was grey after the rain from the water of the meadow streams which had flowed into it. Lost in thought, Katharina's gaze followed the branches carried along by the river – carried away – as the previous summer had gone, as the spring and as Hieronymus had gone and had not returned, not returned ...

An unexpected rustling sound caused Katharina to rise. Behind her on the narrow road leading to the bank, three riders had stopped. As she moved back several steps, she recognized the king with his servants. He jumped from his horse, threw the reins to the others and approached her respectfully.

"My young lady, may I accompany you back into town?" he asked her with his lovely accent. Katharina only nodded. They returned through the Elster Gate back into town where the townsmen were standing around. They shook their heads and looked after the strange pair. The king asked her about her future, about her flight from the convent, about her plans.

"I will marry," said Katharina with a firm voice.

"Lucky man," he said. In front of the entrance of the Cranach house, Christian remained standing. "Beautiful country. Beautiful women," he said and pulled a ring from his finger. Without hesitation, he reached for Katharina's hand and put the ring on it. "A keepsake." Then he stepped up to the door and disappeared into the house before Katharina could think of a way to thank him. In the evening she saw him again sitting at the table with Cranach and Luther. A day later, he rode away very early. Perplexed, she studied the ring.

"Pray that God guides your king – He will need it," said Barbara.

That night in the room which she shared with Ave, Katharina dreamed: There was a narrow road between blooming trees and in the distance a figure came toward her. The nearer it came, the clearer it became. It was Hieronymus. He spread his arms and it seemed to Katharina that he was calling. She wanted to run toward him but then the picture dissolved. The trees were now bare like huge skeletons at the edge of the road and she awoke.

Outside, it had frozen. The first snow was blowing down the street. Katharina got up but before she began to work, she walked out into the street. Wrapped in the warm coat which Barbara had given her as a gift, she went through the deserted town to the Elster Gate. There she stood and stared at the landscape lost in the grey of the early day. No one was coming.

In the evening, she sat with Barbara and the children by the hearth. While the others chatted happily, Katharina sat with her lips tightly closed.

"Roll on the spring. The streets are so covered with snow,"said Barbara.

"As I came past the birch forest by the gate yesterday morning, the naked trunks stood as ... as the women in the pictures of Meister Lucas. A veil of fog floated around them like the transparent clothes which he paints around their bodies. They are so slim and beautiful ..." Barbara smiled as Katharina talked. The two of them sat at the window and embroidered children's blouses. But Katharina put down her work in her lap and looked thoughtfully in front of her. "How does Meister Lucas know what women look like?" she asked suddenly. Barbara laughed out loud and looked around her. The door to the stairs was closed tightly. No one was listening,

"He is married, Katharina," she whispered. "So you ...? And he knows ... ?" Noisily came the sound of the servants voices below. Barbara was blushing under her gold-embroidered cap. "You will experience it when Hieronymus comes for you and celebrates your wedding with you."

The bells of St Mary's church began to ring. Barbara laid the little shirts to one side and went into the kitchen. A short time later she called back:

"Katharina, the tailor is here. We want you to try on your garment."

Wrapped in soft material, Katharina stood in front of the window. Barbara tugged at the sleeve and pulled at the back. The tailor crawled around on the floor and pinned the hem, lisping at the same time without stopping:

"What finery, mein Fräulein! What finery! You could be a princess, Fräulein. Up in the castle they are hardly better dressed. You also have the right posture, Fräulein von Bora. So upright and straight. Perhaps you should make an appearance at the castle."

"Oh, John, won't you stop talking," interrupted the mistress of the house. "Someone like Katharina fits much better into a rich townsman's house. Or are you trying to say that the Cranachs live more shabbily than those in the castle?" The excited tailor jumped up, went to and fro between the women and let out a flood of explanations as he tried to correct the wrong impression he had given. Barbara laughed happily as Katharina looked down at herself. The expensive material which Meister Lucas had given her as a gift slipped through her fingers, stroking her skin.

"What would Hieronymus say to this?"

"You are dreaming, Katharina! Come, take off the garment so that John can sew the seams. Let's go into the garden with the children."

---

The silver birches in front of the Elster Gate took on a delicate green hue. The house of the painter had over eighty rooms, and it was full of noise as usual. At the front in the print room, the machines were thumping. On the yard side, in the painter's studio, the artisans called to each other and with loud groans shoved the heavy props from one corner to another. In the centre of the room stood the portrait of the unfortunate King of Denmark, half finished. The apprentices worked on the wooden panels of an altar. The maids worked in the kitchen and, between the shelves of the pharmacy, young Doktor Basilius hurried back and forth, stirring the substances in the glasses and crushing dried herbs into a fine powder. His wife Ave was helping him.

Katharina lay in bed with a fever. From afar, noise reached her ears. In the midst of the noise, she heard steps drawing closer. The mistress of the house walked in with a beaker and sat by the sick woman. "Drink, Katharina. This is an aromatic wine. Doktor Basilius has sent it for you. We are concerned about you." Katharina sat up and drank obediently. Then she fell back, exhausted. Her eyes looked empty. Barbara remained sitting. "Would you like to come to the table for the evening meal? Meister Lucas has just returned from Torgau and will certainly have much to talk about."

"I will try," said Katharina softly.

"I have to go now." The sick woman nodded and closed her eyes. Barbara stood for another moment by the bed and sighed.

At supper, Meister Lucas lifted up a mug and drank to Katharina:

"Well, Fräulein von Bora, you should be moving on in the spring. Is it not already over a year since you left the convent? We are glad for you although you are certainly a significant help in the house, not to mention the pharmacy. And we need you for, if I'm not mistaken, your friend Ave will not be able to help us much longer because she will soon celebrate the baptism of a child." Cranach smiled at Basilius while Ave blushed. "So there are now only two nuns whom we need to marry off," he continued with good humour. "Is this not true? Elsa von Canitz, who is living with her sister and ..." Katharina grew pale.

"Have some more venison, Meister Lucas," his wife interjected. Cranach set the mug down and raised his eyebrows. He looked at Katharina.

"If I have said anything wrong, please forgive me." Katharina felt his look piercing her. She tried to get up but Barbara pushed her back on the chair. Silent and pale, she looked out at the lively table where jokes and laughter were being shared.

After everyone became tired from eating so heartily, the door flew open and a dark figure burst in. The conversation stopped immediately.

"Doktor Martinus," called the master of the house, "Come in and sit down with us. I'm sure there is still some wine in the jug." But Luther remained standing in the dark corner of the room. He looked anxiously at the faces of those who sat at the table. His gaze stopped for a moment at Ave and then moved to his friend.

"Meister Lucas, I have received news. Things are steaming! They are boiling! The peasants are reading the Gospel. They demand the Kingdom of God. It drives me to..." [36] Breathing heavily, Luther let himself fall into a chair beside Cranach and the two fell into earnest conversation.

Without anyone noticing, Katharina slipped away to her room. She rummaged around in her bag which lay beside her bed and pulled out her rosary. Kneeling on the floor, she let the pearls slip through her fingers and prayed in a whisper as the tears streamed down her face, *Ave Maria gratia plena ...* Hail Mary, full of grace, the Lord is with thee ... The next morning, she arose with difficulty and went into the pharmacy. Barbara found her there tying the herbs into bundles and looked anxiously into her face. Katharina's eyes were red, her cheeks pale, and her mouth defiantly closed. In the evening when a messenger from Rector Glatz[37] asked for Katharina, the mistress of the house told him at the door that she was sick. The messenger left a letter.

———————————

The town clerk, Reichenbach, walked to and fro in front of Katharina clothed in his counsellor's gown. She sat on a chair with her back to the window, her hands tightly clasped.

"Katharina, you know that we received you as a daughter when you came to Wittenberg. Thus, it is our responsibility to be concerned about your future. We would have liked to give you in marriage to Hieronymus, for you were attracted to each other. Both of you are pious and honest – even though he was actually too young for someone like you. But now a year has passed. There is no news of him. And a valiant man, the rector of the university … "

Katharina shifted her weight.

"What do you have to say?" Reichenbach asked.

"I do not want to be disobedient, good sir, but I beg you, wait some more. It is easy to lose a message between Nurenberg and Wittenberg. And perhaps, perhaps the family was too taken aback."

"That is very likely true," sighed Reichenbach. He stopped in front of Katharina and looked at her. "Please, Katharina, don't hang your heart too much on this one hope!"

She looked up. His eyes were full of kindness as they looked down at her. And yet fear choked her throat and she stuttered helplessly. "I will try."

"Do you feel comfortable in the house of the painter?" She nodded. "Do you see Doktor Luther there occasionally?"

"Yes."

"I will ask him for his advice." Katharina nodded again.

"Please tell Doktor Glatz that he should still wait – this summer, this autumn."

---

"Do you believe, Katharina, that you are the first? We have all experienced it." Shocked, Katharina stood still.

"But surely not you, Frau Barbara?" They went through the garden in front of the inner wall of the town, the baskets on their arms full of cherries.

"Me too, Katharina … To be sure, I was still much younger than you are, barely fourteen years old, when I got to know a boy, with black, full locks of hair. Oh, it was only a short time, then he was gone. One of the travellers who came to the large markets.[38] He did not return although he promised me he would." She stood and looked out at the swallows chasing each other in the blue sky. "Should I, a child of rich parents, perhaps have gone with him? What choice did I have? I accepted the man whom my parents gave me. He died before the wedding. I had to grieve as though I was a widow. And I was then relieved when Cranach, an imposing man, came along."

"I believe it would have been better if I had remained in the convent."

Barbara shook her head vigorously. "Just because a man has disappeared, never to be seen again? No, Katharina. You are ungrateful." Katharina's eyes filled with tears and she hung her head so that no one could see them.

"Perhaps God is punishing me for my sins," she said very softly. Along the wall, the women encountered the younger Cranach children. Young Lucas, earnest and tall, followed little Barbara. Baby Margaret screamed. With an affectionate smile, her mother took her out of the arms of the maid and gave the basket to the maid. Katharina stood there silently. Suddenly, she realized that she could actually forget Hieronymus.

———————

"I will not accept him."

"Are you too proud, Fräulein von Bora?"

"No. I am not proud but I did not flee the convent to enter another prison. It must be someone else." The cathedral head Nicholaus von Amsdorf[39] sighed. Somewhat indignantly, he looked at Katharina who sat in front of him on a high chair in his half empty study. Amsdorf was going to Magdeburg.

"What do you expect of me?"

"Tell Doktor Luther that I will not accept Glatz."

"He is an honest man and represents the new teaching with conviction."

"You don't know him."

"Oh, yes, I do. To be sure – Hieronymus Baumgaertner was a different proposition. But – what will become of you if you do not marry?"

"I know that Hieronymus isn't coming back. I am also ready to accept another man. If you – or even Doktor Martin Luther — were to ask for me. But Glatz, I will not accept." Katharina got up.

"Can I show you the way out?"

"Thank you, Meister von Amsdorf."

Katharina bade  farewell quietly and returned to the Cranach house. There she sat at the kitchen table and, in the dim light of a candle whose wick had almost burned down, she wrote a letter to her friend Elsa:

> I have to fight hard, dear sister, to prevent them from giving me Glatz, a small and stingy man who has no sense of humor. I trust that Doktor Martin Luther will not take away the freedom which he helped us win. Would God really want me to marry this pathetic man? Never before have I been as uncertain about what God wants from me. The Reverend Mother taught us that, when the devil sows doubt into the heart, you need only pray. Now my heart is sometimes completely despondent and I would like to be able to pray again as I did then. I read in your letter, dear Elsa, that you are also experiencing great difficulties with your relatives. Other sisters have been more fortunate. Ave is already a happy young mother cradling her little boy. I hear even Magdalena has married. So God is

leading each of us. And I pray with many tears that you and I also succeed in reaching the right goal. Dear sister, let us trust that this will happen. Send me news to the house of the painter.
Greetings in true sisterly love, Katharina von Bora,
In the house of the painter, Lucas Cranach in Wittenberg.

She sealed the letter and the next day she gave it to the messenger who carried letters and bills from the Cranach house throughout Saxony. He promised conscientiously to deliver it to Fräulein Elsa von Canitz in the Leipzig suburb of Zu der Eiche (To the Oak).

---

"Luther has received bad news," Barbara told to the women as she allowed her coat to be taken. "The raving peasants do not want to listen to his admonition. It is said that he has become sick with anger." [40] The multitude of sounds from the house drifted into the room. Katharina laid her needle work aside.

"Should I bring him something out of the pharmacy?"

"Yes," said Barbara. "Bring him some cake from the bakery, as well. And wine. The poor man is carrying the load of the whole world on his shoulders. Who would not become sick?"

"I know another medicine for him ... "

"What medicine do you mean?"

"He should get married."

"But who would have him? The income from his preaching could not feed a family. He is rotting as a living corpse alone in the empty monastery."

Thoughtfully, Katharina went down into the bakery. There the maids were busy cleaning the copper pots. But no laughter rang through the stairway as one normally heard. As Katharina pushed open the heavy door, she saw old Marie sitting at the table, her eyes red from crying. The other maid went silently about her work.

"Marie, what has happened?" Katharina had often joked with Marie and related things that had happened in the convent and about the long periods of fasting. But this time she did not answer but blew her nose in her apron.

"Her niece," Lisa whispered, "Have you not heard, Fräulein? The Count of Mansfeld has killed virtually everyone in our village. Her brothers, her sons, my father – all dead, all dead. And they have taken the youngest of her sons away captive ... " Lisa's voice failed her. The old woman began to scream:

"Don't whisper. Don't whisper. Say it." She got up from the table and tore handfuls of hair from her head. "Say it. They have him. They are torturing him. They are putting him to the rack. Oh, the good lad, the little one. Oh, no, no, no!" The maids ran out of the door. Lisa tried to calm the raving woman. But with a distorted face and wildly gesticulating arms, she attacked Katharina verbally. "Yes, Fräulein, yes. That's what they are doing – these Christian princes, these servants of the devil! That's what they are doing to us. We are only dirt! We are just peasants! We are only animals! Only good enough to work until our bones break. Yes, until they sweat more than their animals would sweat. And woe to them if they rebel! Kick them. Use the sword. To the rack. Grill the young man – my dear son with blond hair – until his skin bursts and splits. Until he screams: 'Mother, help.' Until he screams! Aye ... "

The horrible lament of the old woman echoed in the high vaulted rooms. The door flew noisily open. Meister Lucas stood in the doorway.

"What is wrong, old woman? What do you mean by this yelling?"

"Meister, save him!" She crumbled to the floor and clutched the feet of the painter with both hands. "Save him! They are going to torture him, the child, the dear child." Cranach tried in vain to push the old woman to the side. In the process, he looked at her face with great attentiveness.

"But why did he go with the peasants? Why did he allow himself to be misled?"

"They didn't know any better. Luther told them ... They read it in the Bible and they believed that the Holy Spirit was with them ... " Lisa tried to explain: "At the market there was a trader from our village who told her about it. Everyone is dead and the youngest has been taken captive ... " Katharina took the cake and slipped out of the pantry. The sound of old Marie's howling followed her right onto the street. To have a son ... and then war ... and then torture.

A cold wind drove drizzling rain down the street. The branches already had rigid buds. Man and nature waited for the sun. Could summer ever return after so much blood had soaked into the earth? Lost in thought, Katharina went across the street and over the yard to the Black Monastery. It was quiet – as if everyone had died around the large old house. The door was slightly ajar. Katharina knocked and walked in. From the dimly lit entrance hall, she saw a man walking to and fro. She remained standing and waited. However, it was only after she shyly wished him a good evening that he saw her and came toward her. His face was pale; his dark eyes looked wild.

"Is it you, Fräulein von Bora? What are you bringing? Do you have more frightening news for me?

Have the armies of the devil broken into Saxony? Have more churches been burned down and innocent people murdered – and are they still saying, Luther wanted it to happen?"

"I bring you greetings from the house of Cranach and some cake with a little wine to strengthen you."

"Ha!" The door behind Katharina's back closed so that she stood with Luther in virtual darkness. "Why do you bring me wine for strength? Whom do you want to strengthen? Do you not know, Fräulein von Bora, who is standing before you? Here, here, see my hands! See the blood dripping from them. Was I not with them when they stormed Weinsberg and burned women and children in the fire? Do I not commit murder daily? Do I not plunder and throw the statues of saints on the refuse pile? I have given them the pure unadulterated Gospel to read – and what do they read? Revolt! Murder!"

Luther again began to rush to and fro like one being hunted. He no longer spoke to Katharina. He was yelling at the walls.

"The devil leads the armies. The devil leads them! They have read the Gospel of Christ – and the devil has explained it to them." He remained standing in front of Katharina and whispered: "That Gospel also motivated you, Fräulein von Bora. As you read in the convent: 'A Christian is a perfectly free lord of all, subject to none ... ,' you said, 'So I can go out and leave this servitude behind.' Now the peasants say the same but they do not understand that there must be order. They did not want to pay their tithes any longer. They gather in gangs, murder, plunder ... and are murdered. I am the least blessed of all preachers. I have brought the revolt into the land – and now it is killing me. Yes, it should kill me." Luther collapsed in a heap on a bench. "They have all deserted me, Fräulein von Bora, everyone. They are all against me: the princes and the peasants, the pope and the emperor, the learned and the beggars … So then I will go my way to the end, to the bitter end."

Somewhere the rafters groaned. Katharina dared not move.

"But you too … you too have been deserted," he said. "I wrote to Baumgaertner some time ago, last year. Recently an answer came by messenger from Nurenberg. From his father. He prohibited his son from marrying you. His son didn't want to obey. But his mother almost died of grief. So he renounced you. Therefore, you are free, Fräulein von Bora. You did not want Glatz. You communicated this to me through Amsdorf. What is left for you? I don't know."

So as not to remain standing in the passage, Katharina went ahead into the gloomy dining room of the former monastery. There she placed her basket on the table. Luther followed her. She tried to speak but was unable to do so. It was quiet for a long time. Finally, she uttered a few words:

"Yes, Doktor, I too have been abandoned. You are right but not entirely. And you too still have – friends. See here! See what Frau Barbara has sent. Take! Eat!"

Amazed, Luther remained standing in front of Katharina. He looked at her. A thought appeared to come to him for he suddenly began to laugh, loud and uproariously. He hit his fist on the table and then on his forehead.

"You have correctly said, 'Take! Eat!' Yes, Fräulein von Bora. You have spoken correctly. As the raven came to Elijah when the prophet despaired,[41] so you came to me. Now I am in despair. The devil laughs at me. But he shall laugh still more. They shall ridicule me all the more, all of those who wait for Doktor Martin Luther to go to hell. I now know what I will do before I die. I will marry you."

Katharina's hand groped in the semi-darkness for a chair. "You are silent, Fräulein von Bora. You are right. What I have done is too frightening. 'A Christian is a perfectly free lord of all, subject to none ... ' I had better die alone."

"No." Luther appeared not to have heard. He laid his head on his arm and sat unmoving at the table. The door creaked in the wind. Katharina pulled her chair closer and sat down beside Luther. "No," she repeated.

He straightened up. "What are you trying to say? Shall I not die alone? – But you are still so young."

"I told Amsdorf, if you want to marry me ... "

After a while, Luther stretched out his hand and laid it on hers. "Do you truly want to do this? Have you truly thought about it? I do not expect to live much longer. All I would have to leave to you are my two silver chalices, then at least you would have something in your widowhood. Fräulein von Bora ... Katie ... My Katie?"

As she returned to the house of Cranach, Katharina first slipped into the bakery. Old Marie was still sitting at the table weeping. Katharina stood beside her. "God will be merciful."

"No, Fräulein, no. He is merciful only to the rich."

Confused, Katharina climbed up to her room. That night, she lay awake and listened. It was quiet in the house. Outside the wind blew. She wondered if Luther was still pacing to and fro. She sighed at the thought of that large empty building in which he would lay his straw mattress anywhere. Virtually in a dream, she saw his pale face, his disorderly black curly hair, and heard his voice as close as her own heart, 'My Katie?' Then she fell asleep.

———————

Katharina stood beside Barbara Cranach in the worship service in the second row beneath the pulpit. Bugenhagen preached. "And so we stand before our

Father in heaven not with our hands full. We cannot say, 'See Lord, how great are our works, what great things we have ... ' " Katharina looked at her hands. They had become strong since she had begun working in the house of Cranach. "For it is all by grace, the grace of our Lord Jesus Christ. "

Around her, people breathed deeply, blew their noses and cleared their throats. The worshippers stood packed close together. But Katharina's thoughts left the Wittenberg congregation behind and followed the man journeying somewhere through the land – so unlike the spring which is mild and bright. He threw lightning and thunder into the crowd which surrounded him and pressed in on him and perhaps also turned its back on him. Would they listen to him – the peasants, who with scythe and flail had gone forth? Would they listen to him or would he shout to no avail?

"Amen. And the peace of God, which is higher than all violence." Katharina bowed her head, trying to collect herself. The Cranach children beside her became restless. Barbara sat on a stool and held the baby on her lap. Little Lucas pulled his little sister's ponytail. The Meister was not with them, but Hans, the oldest, stood with his brow furrowed, beside his mother.

As the congregation began to sing, Katharina cringed. What would the Abbot of Pforta say about this singing? Everyone held the notes as long as they thought they should and the women's voices trembled like nightingales. There was no standard and no longer any order. Katharina looked around her. Behind her a merchant's fat wife sang with raised head and eyes looking heavenward,

If the Lord himself had not been on our side
Now may Israel say
If the Lord himself had not been on our side

When men rose up against us.
They had swallowed us up quick.

After the Lord's Prayer was said and the blessing spoken, the children ran outside, relieved. Katharina smiled at the merchant's wife and took little Anna by the hand. It took some time for her to make her way through the throng of the townswomen dressed in their Sunday best.

"Why was Meister Lucas not in church?" asked Katharina as they went back across the market place to the Cranach home.

"Why, indeed? He says that when he works at home and hears the bells ring, that is the best service of worship for him. That's how men are, whether old believers or Lutherans, they gladly leave churchgoing to the women!"

While the housewife went to the kitchen where the maids were preparing the Sunday roast, Katharina went into the studio. She found Meister Lucas in front of an altar picture. In the crowd which had gathered under the cross of Christ, he was shaping an individual face. He was so preoccupied that he did not hear Katharina. She stood behind him and followed his work. As he moved his hand a little to the side, she let out a short scream. Lucas turned:

"You startled me, Katharina!"

"But that is ... that is old Marie!"

"Yes, perhaps." In the middle of the soldiers with their faces distorted by hatred and murder, the painter had placed the despairing woman. Her wide-open eyes looked up at the tormented Saviour. Not far away – half finished – the Mother of God leaned at the foot of the cross. A journeyman had worked on it. Strangely detached, she turned toward the observer. But not old Marie! What need screamed from her face! She stood in the midst of the weapons and the scornful laughter of the soldiers. The mouths of the men stood open. Their eyes rolled under their bushy brows. They gesticulated wildly with their swords and spears and could not get enough blood.

"Meister Lucas – Who are you painting?"

"The peasants, Katharina, and the soldiers – they are all alike in their lust for blood."

He laid his paint brush down on the table, took a step back and studied the throng.

"Luther is with the peasants."[42] Katharina said.

"I know."

"And if they … "

"They will not dare to lay a hand on him. The Emperor and the empire could not kill him."

Katharina sighed. "But he says he wants to die." The painter turned and smiled benignly.

"Do you not know how to prevent that?" Katharina blushed.

"I wish he was back again."

"God will keep His hand over him." Katharina folded her hands over her chest and wished she had prayed more fervently in church.

"Come. Frau Barbara will be needing us." They left the studio and went across the yard. The little girls, Barbara and Anne, ran laughing toward them. Katharina breathed heavily.

"If the Lord himself had not been on our side … "

---

They came secretly. They went away again secretly: the Cranachs, in good humour and speaking happily; Pastor Bugenhagen, serious and earnest; at his side, Justus Jonas[43] with tears in his eyes. They left the door of the Black Monastery open behind them. Warm summer air flowed into the old building. Katharina looked after them as they went across the yard out to the street and turned left toward town. The people living in the area had no idea yet what had happened. However, when the friends reached home – they would certainly pick up their pens so that everyone would know it – women in the market, traders, emperor, kings and bishops: the monk and the nun have wed[44]

She remained standing in the doorway. The lime trees blossomed between the old walls. In the middle of the yard stood a young pear tree which had begun to yield fruit. The house behind her was already in the shade. Stale air came out of the corners. On the table the jug of wine from which they had drank after the short wedding ceremony remained standing. And somewhere in the dark rooms in a brown robe, broad and large, pacing nervously to and fro, her man waited for her.

A magpie flew up with a loud screech and disappeared over the roof tops. Wolf, the servant, shuffled in from the kitchen and cleared the cups.

"Good night, Wolf," said Katharina.

"Good night, Fräul—ahem, Frau Doktor." She heard him staggering back into the kitchen. Then she shut the door and turned around.

She found Luther in his room where two straw mattresses lay side by side. Both were covered with gleaming white linen from the chest of Frau Barbara. The straw smelled fresh.

"Now, Frau Doktor ... " They were quiet for a while. Katharina slowly opened the ties of her cap and took it off. Long blond plaits fell down her back. Luther smiled. He came over to her and gently stroked her hair with his hand.

"How beautiful!"

"Yes," she said. "It has grown during these two years." She began to loosen her bodice as Luther nervously shifted his weight from one foot to the other.

"Katie, I am ... I have never ... I mean touched a woman. You must forgive me. I am certainly not made of stone but how it should be done? "

"If the horses in the barn know, don't you think Doktor that we will also be able?"

"Yes, God has willed it and has taught the animals. You are right, dear nun. So He will also show us." Katharina laid her brown outer garment neatly over the trunk.

"I have suffered like others under the illusion of the devil," continued Luther and began gesticulating wildly. "I told myself, it is not permitted and it is a sin." Katharina stood in a long white night gown in the middle of the room. Startled, she looked at him. Could it be that it was not God's but the devil's work that they were here together? Trembling, Luther stood still. "It is not good that man should be alone. Genesis, Chapter 2," he whispered.

"Yes," said Katharina relieved. "You know that better than I, Doktor. But, should you not perhaps. remove your outer garments?"

---

"Katie, there must have been 8,000 killed in Frankenhausen. 8,000 — can you picture that? No. No, you can't. I cannot sleep. They come at me – 8,000! An immense crowd. Always more coming. They crawl out of every hole like ants – with distorted faces, shattered skulls, carrying their amputated limbs under their arms. No. I cannot sleep, Katie. How can I sleep?"

"You have said and written that it is right if the princes kill them like dogs. You have written that it is God's will."

"Yes, Katie, yes – but 8,000 and countless others whom they torture and roast as though they want to fill heaven with their screams. Oh, God! What have I done!"

"Sleep, Martin, sleep!"

"But they're coming. They leap upon me with their scythes and halberds. I wish they would kill me. I wish I was dead! Oh, God in heaven!"

Katie reached out her hand and stroked her husband's sweating forehead. She listened to the sounds of the night. the frightful wailing of old Marie. Had it not yet died away? She was filled with horror. A feeling of horror constricted her throat. With a start she sat up.

"Listen, Martin, leave the battle fields! Peace has come. The dead are dead. It is past. There is peace and we want to keep it that way. What is dead, is before God. We are on earth. Tomorrow we will go into the garden. There is much to do and you have to help. A bough of the cherry tree has broken off. The cucumbers are getting ripe and in the herb garden weeds are growing. Have you seen how the roses are blooming? Wolf must help me repair the roof of the goose shed; the day before yesterday it rained in. Yes, and the water man brought the barrels. I will begin to brew beer. It is time to do that. We cannot keep buying that expensive Torgau beer. But my beer won't be ready before the celebration meal to which you invited people. For that we have to rely on Herr Koppe. So, write to him right away tomorrow, Doktor, so that he brings us some – our friends should have a good time in this dilapidated house. Will you do it?" Luther turned on his side and sighed,

"Yes, Lord Katie."

———————————

Wednesday after Corpus Christi—1525.

"To the gentle and wise Leonhard Koppe, townsman from Torgau, my dear sir and friend.

Grace and Peace in Christ!

God has suddenly and without warning caught me in the bands of holy matrimony, the confirmation of which I will observe by throwing a banquet on Tuesday. So that my father and mother and all my good friends may celebrate, my Lord Katie and I would kindly ask you to bring us a barrel of the best Torgau beer that you can get. Charge it to me and bring it here. I will repay you everything.

May God lead you. Amen. Martin Luther."

Koppe's wagon swayed early in the morning through the Elbe Gate. Katie heard his call on the street and hastily removed her apron. In the yard, Koppe stopped and called loudly:

"Hey! Hello! Where's the bride?" In the dining room, two old people sat silently without moving. Katie ran past them.

"Father. Mother. This is Merchant Koppe from Torgau!" – and opened the door. Smiling, she presented them to the man who had rescued her from the convent. Cheerfully, Koppe spread out his arms, then stepped back startled and bowed deeply:

"Frau Doktor, my deepest respect!" He could hardly keep from laughing as Katie looked down embarassed. Luther walked to the wagon and helped Frau Koppe down, puffing as she attempted to straighten the clothes she was wearing.

"Oh, my dear nun," she called at the sight of Katie. "How good you look!" From town, other guests approached.

"Come into the house. Come in!" Luther directed them inside with inviting, outstretched arms.

He presented his guests to the two older people. His mother looked quietly at her hands folded in her lap. His father's eyes moved quickly from one face to another.

"These, Father, are our friends. First of all, you see the valiant merchant Koppe, who brought my bride out of the convent." Katie hurried again into the kitchen. Veronica, known for her cooking throughout Wittenberg, had organized a whole host of maids who had come from the homes of their friends.

"Will you stir the soup so it doesn't burn? Who told you to throw in the garlic cloves, useless thing? You're to cut chives in small rings, not in strips!" So she marched to and fro in the kitchen scolding as she went. Meanwhile Katie laid out the silver borrowed from the Cranachs. The soup steamed. The roast hissed over the fire. At the door, new guests were being greeted with a loud "Hello." People called for the bride. She straightened her bonnet, wiped her face with her apron and stumbled outside. Cranach's voice roared out of the entrance hall toward her. Luther sat at the small side of the table, his father to his right, his mother to his left, and with strong retorts, responded to the jests which his friends threw at him. Satisfied, his father smiled.

The ringing of bells interrupted the conversation. The guests formed a festive procession.

"Oh, Katie, look at yourself!" Barbara Cranach shook her head and tugged and pulled at the bodice, at the bonnet, at the hoop — until Luther became impatient.

"Leave her alone, Frau Barbara. To me she is beautiful enough." Katie took a deep breath and walked to his side. Her face was flushed from the heat in the kitchen but also from an inner fire. Behind her went his parents: old Luther in a brown robe, proud and upright; his mother stooped at his side. As the procession neared the church, the doors of the houses flew open. Women and maids hung out of the windows. They pointed out to their children the monk and the nun celebrating their wedding. And what the townsmen mockingly said behind their backs, the students called out aloud:

"See here, a new age is upon us. Soon now the Antichrist will rule."

Katie heard the jeers through the ringing of the bells. But she held her head even higher and walked without hesitation at the side of her husband to the shadow of the church.[45]

———————————

With a powerful motion, Katie opened the door of the Black Monastery and walked into the yard. A sunny summer morning lay before her. She let out a quiet cry of joy as she felt the warmth of the early sun on her arms. But there was no time for singing and praying. The maid came sleepily across the yard and awaited instructions. In the barns the poultry made noises. And behind her came Luther through the entrance hall. His eyes grew moist as he saw her standing in the doorway, her dress tucked in, her sleeves pushed up.

"Now, Katie. Will you prove again how right King Solomon was when he said, 'The man who has been given a capable wife has something much more precious than any jewel?' "[46] But the look on his face, as his eyes glided over her naked arms and ankles also indicated something else beyond his satisfaction regarding her diligence.

"Oh," said Katie, a little embarrassed, "when a man has slept so well! " In quiet agreement they nodded at each other. Wolf shuffled over. He was obviously not so pleased that the sun shone into the house so early, since the Frau Doktor had moved in. "Listen, Wolf, you have to help me today in the brewery. But first I must bring the chickens some water. And I also hear the goats bleating, wanting to get out. Come, Herr Doktor, I must show you the kid that was born yesterday ... " She grabbed Luther's sleeve and pulled him over the doorway into the open air. Beside the entrance in freshly dug earth, stood a young rosebush. Luther stood there and meditated.

"How beautifully it blooms!" Katie turned on her heel and clapped her hands laughing.

"Truly, now Doktor Luther has his rose alive and perfuming the front of the house." And she whirled away across the yard.

At that moment, a wagon rattled in from the street. Katie didn't need to look up to know that it was Koppe.

"Hey! Hello!" called the driver and threw his cap into the air.

"Old friend, what do you bring us today?"

"A nun, Herr Doktor, a nun!" Katie laughed aloud but, with a mischievous smile, the driver gently lifted the canvas covering. He had many barrels piled up on one another but in their midst, crowded into a very small space, sat a white figure with a black shawl around her, shivering in spite of the warm morning sun.

"Aunt Lena!" Stunned, Katie rung her hands. "Aunt Lena!" She could hardly wait until Koppe had lifted the frail woman from the wagon.

"Did I not say, Doktor, 'a nun'?"

Katie hugged her aunt and Luther, touched, looked over from the white roses to the white-clad woman. With a bow, he walked over to her:

"Fräulein Magdalena von Bora – for it can only be you – it seems to me that my wife has never hugged me as passionately as she has you … " Katie turned around indignantly. "… until yesterday," Luther hastened to add. "Welcome, precious Fräulein, to our home." Magdalena did not dare to look into the face of the famous man.

"So then," called Koppe, who had swung himself back onto the wagon seat, "where is my payment for this trip?"

"If I still had the twenty gulden which the Archbishop of Mainz gave us as a wedding gift, I would pay you," Luther called back cheerfully. "But I gave it back to the old fox. So come down again, dear Koppe, and eat and drink with us. You have been on the road for a long time already." As Luther mentioned the twenty gulden, Katie blushed and looked quickly to the side. But she concluded that it was not the right moment to explain to Luther the whereabouts of the money. The gulden rested safely in the bottom drawer of Katie's chest until there would be a good reason to spend them.

"I must be going, Doktor, but on my return trip I will come and expect you to butcher the fatted calf." The horses started up. The wagon moved forward and turned, and the women waved until he disappeared along the street to town.

"Come in. Come in, Aunt Lena. Wolf, bring us milk from the kitchen. Where is Greta? She must now look after the chickens. We need bread, Wolf. Oh, Aunt Lena, tell us, tell us! Did he also get you out of the convent by night? No, probably not. There are already so many who have left. What is the Reverend Mother doing now – without her children? Oh, she wasn't bad.

After all, she was my aunt too. But what did she know about us? You are so thin. I will take care of you. Now, tell me!"

Chuckling, Luther cast another look at the two and then went up the stairs to his study. Katie remained seated beside her aunt who was still shaking but who had begun slowly and haltingly to talk. As she listened, Katie took a mental measurement of the table. Almost every day another diner was added: foreigners and friends, relatives and the persecuted. They came and didn't leave again.

"You will sit beside me, Aunt Lena," Katie decided.

"I don't eat much, my child."

"I know that but I don't know how I will feed everyone else." Her aunt looked closely into her face.

"You look strong and healthy, Katie. You will make it. And I will do whatever I can do to help you."

"Yes, Aunt Lena, thank you."

---

"Wolf! Greta!" Katie's voice sounded hard and shrill through the house. She slammed her basket down behind the door and threw her coat over a chair. It was raining outside – the water ran over her face and dripped from her coat to the floor. Greta took one look at the face of her mistress and busied herself with removing the vegetables from the basket and carrying them into the kitchen. Katie stumbled up the stairs and tore open the door of her aunt's room. Magdalena sat in the semi-darkness by the window and sewed a bonnet.

"What's wrong, child?" With lips pressed tightly together, Katie stood shaking. Her aunt waited patiently. "What's wrong, Katie? Take a chair. Sit down!"

"I have to prepare supper."

"First tell me what has happened." Katie collapsed into a chair. She tried to speak but could not.

"These women. These vile mouths!" With difficulty, she fought against the sobs that choked her. "I went across to the market and met Melanchthon's wife with her maids. She greeted me condescendingly, the pretentious goose. I wanted to go on but she pulled my sleeve and whispered, 'There is a new song in Wittenberg – Did you know that?' Naturally, I said, 'No' and wished her a good day. Then she laughed and let me go. At the edge of the market, not far from the house of Cranach, some students stood and sang to a lute. They sang ... "

"Katie, calm yourself!"

"They sang:

'The monk and his lover,
Wallowed under cover;
Whence Antichrist was given birth,
Isn't that the cause for mirth?'[47]

"I don't recall any more how the rest of it went but it was horrible, Aunt Lena. It was horrible ... "

Magdalena sighed and laid aside her sewing. The women sat together in silence. It became dark in the room.

"Why do they do it, Aunt Lena?"

"Oh, Katie, they don't understand. I didn't understand at first either. But I thought about it. I thought about it a lot. And finally I recognized that Luther was right. But these foolish fellows don't want to recognize it. And because they are cowards, they ridicule you. "

Out of the large hall of the monastery, a song came to their ears: *Christe, du Lamm Gottes...* (O Christ, thou Lamb of God, that takest away the sin of the world ...)

three men's voices sang out and then suddenly – silence.

"On Sunday we will celebrate the Mass for the first time in German," said Katie. "It will be difficult for me but the melodies are beautiful, aren't they?" The singing by the three powerful voices resumed and this time they carried the melody through to the end: *Gib uns deinen Frieden. Amen* (grant us your peace. Amen)

"Amen," repeated Magdalena.

Katie stood up.

"It is best that I don't go out on the street anymore. I can hardly stand this Wittenberg. These narrow walls! One would almost think that I was in the convent. I would rather live somewhere out there – in Lippendorf, you know. There the children could play. "

Magdalena looked up attentively. Katie's face, still wet from her tears, relaxed.

"Yes, we are going to have a child, Aunt Lena. Yes, soon."

"And here you are crying about the songs which some worthless fellows are singing at the market?"

"I am afraid. They are all expecting that something will happen, something horrible, that the Antichrist will be born. Oh, God!"

"I know, Katie, but did not the Doktor show us all that the Antichrist will sit on his throne in Rome and wear three crowns?"

"Yes ... but in spite of that ... Please, Aunt Lena, pray for my child!"

"That I will certainly do, Katie. I am an expert at this," and her aunt laid her sewing aside and folded her hands. Slowly Katie went down into the kitchen. From the hall the voices of the men sounded forth again: *"Kyrie eleison ... Christe eleison ... Kyrie eleison."*[48] Katie hummed along with the melody.

---

Winter came. The wind blew through the cracks around the windows of the Black Monastery. In the kitchen hearth, a fire burned day and night. But in their bedroom, Luther and his wife froze under their thin blankets. Frau Barbara sent over a warm used coat. Katie wore it as she sat at the window sewing a child's shirt with numb fingers. The streets of Wittenberg were empty. On market days, the peasants came into town over the icy roads and brought cabbage and cattle. But by noon, they had already packed up their wagons and driven back home. The children played in their rooms. Only on Sundays when they went to church did people fill the streets and women showed off their furs. In front of the church, several freezing beggars jostled for attention. Katie stopped. A small face with big empty eyes looked up at her. Cheeks hollow. Lips blue. A thin hand extended toward her out of a coat full of holes.

Katie asked, "Where are you from?" Before the child could answer, a woman in rags pushed forward, carrying a nursing baby in her arms.

"Mercy," she whispered and held up the sleeping baby in front of Katie.

"Who are you? Where are you from?"

"Alms, gracious lady, alms. Everything is burned. Everything is dead." An awful fire burned in the woman's eyes. Katie stretched out her hand and tried to take the baby from the mother. "No. No. My child!" Shocked, Katie recoiled. With one arm the unfortunate woman pressed her child to herself. With the other, she struck out blindly around her. A crowd began to form. A number of men placed themselves between Katie and the raving woman. In the crowd of churchgoers they were pushed away from each other.

From inside, one could still hear the scolding of the men and the faint sobbing of the mother. With a powerful voice, Bugenhagen announced the opening verse.

After the worship service, Katie tried to find the woman and the two children again. A biting wind drove small hard flakes into her face. The sky had become almost black. As though out of nowhere, the little girl appeared in front of her. Still silent, she beckoned to Katie. She followed – and found the mother sitting on the ground in the cemetery beside a gravestone, the baby on her arm.

"Come with me," said Katie and shook her shoulder. But the woman didn't move. The snow fell more heavily. Katie looked around for the others with whom she had come to church: Aunt Lena, Barbara Cranach – but no one was there. "Come," called Katie again and grasped the woman with both hands. Lifeless, the woman's body sank against the stone. The baby tumbled from its mother's arm and lay on the snow-covered grave. Its frozen blue lips appeared to be laughing. Katie grabbed the hand of the shivering little girl and rushed as fast as the little one could walk to the Black Monastery. In the kitchen, she washed the child and gave her some milk.

In the evening, Katie sat on her chair beside Luther's writing table. A candle burned. Luther stared into the darkness over his open books .

"They are the children of the peasants who were killed at Frankenhausen. They are wandering around, freezing and starving. What a frightening judgment."

"The little one seems to be a deaf-mute."

"The misery of it."

"Greta will take care of her."

"What's the use?" Luther stood up and stomped to and fro. "I didn't want them to gather in bands. I didn't want ... " Katie sat still and pressed both hands tightly to her body.

"Oh, Doktor, I am afraid for our child. I could not bear it if it should have to suffer hunger."

―――――――――――――

"With God's blessing, my dear splendid wife has born me a son, little Hans Luther. "[49]

The midwife comes once more to the bed of the woman who had just given birth.

"So, Frau Doktor, how are you doing? You did well. After all, you are no longer so young. I'm going now. The little boy is well cared for. And you should rest."

Katie waits until the door is closed. Then she sits up gently.

"Aunt Lena." No one hears her. "Aunt Lena!" The door opens. Luther comes in quietly and bends over her.

"My Katie!"

"Where is our child?"

"They are fighting over who should hold and rock him."

"Ask them to bring him to me, Herr Doktor. I cannot bear to be without my little Hans for a single moment."

"But you should rest now – it was quite an ordeal! Truly, our Lord God has punished you women with childbirth. I was concerned about you when I heard you cry out, Katie!" His black hair hangs tousled over his forehead. She raises her hand and strokes his face.

"I heard your steps the whole time. Yes, it almost tore me apart but now it's past. I am not even tired anymore. Bring me my child!" Exhausted, she falls back. Luther strokes her hand.

"I will tell Greta but nonetheless you have to rest."

He stands up and goes out. Katie listens. The house is full of life. The maids walk up and down. The midwife gives final instructions. Luther calls to Wolf with a loud voice. She perceives that they are preparing for the baptism. Little Hans has to be baptized very quickly, very quickly so that no one can speak of the Antichrist any more. Bugenhagen will come. Cranach and Jonas. Katie smiles. Now everything will be fine. She tries to pray. There is nothing more important that she can do for her child, she thinks. Sleep comes, deep and dreamless, like unconsciousness. When she awakes, it is already dark. It has become quiet in the house. Beside her bed is a box. She pulls herself up and looks inside. His eyes and mouth are pinched tightly together. His sparse black hair falls in locks over his forehead. Her son sleeps.

---

With heavy steps, Katie goes through the garden once more. It is becoming dusk. The sun has sunk into a haze behind the roof of the castle. The animals in the barns seek out a place to sleep. But it seems as if they cannot find peace. The pigs are noisy. The goats kick at each other. A caustic vapour hangs over the town. There is no noise in the streets. Katie remains standing at the wall of the house. Her legs can no longer carry her. High in the night sky, she hears the sound of wild geese gathering to go south. Already?

It is frighteningly quiet in the house. She goes through the kitchen. Greta is clearing away the pots. She is working alone. Everything is dark and empty in the rooms of the students upstairs. Aunt Lena comes down the steps.

"Katie, you must see to Hans – he doesn't want to sleep." The child cries, presses his small head to his mother's breast, his little face flushed. Katie's hands shake. She pushes his little shirt up a little and feels the child's body, his chest, his throat, somewhat more quickly, his shoulders. His skin is soft and rosy, no black spots, no nodes, everything was healthy, healthy ... She presses the child to herself and looks at Magdalena. She nods to her.

"Teeth, Katie, teeth. Nothing worse." Little Hans becomes quiet in the arms of his mother. Drops of sweat stand on his forehead and fall on her hand. He goes to sleep.

Later, Katie sits beside Luther's writing desk in front of the spinning wheel. But her hands lie passively in her lap.

"What is wrong, Lord Katie? Have you become lazy? Do you have enough linen in the cupboard already? Are there no nuts to crack? Idleness is the beginning of all vice. A lazy wife is a punishment of the Lord ... " Luther talks and talks. He talks against the silence and against fear.

"Do you truly believe, Herr Doktor, that we must remain here when everyone else has fled?"

"Don't you trust God, Katie?' She sighs and presses her hand on her bulging stomach.

"Our child moves so much, Herr Doktor."

"That means it will come into this world healthy."

"We have the plague in our house," retorts Katie.

"Katie, Katie ... "

He tosses his quill aside angrily.

"If you want to go, then go! I will stay." With his open hand, he smacks the Bible which lies before him on the table. "Even if a thousand fall by your side and ten thousand on your right, it will not come near you."[50] Katie weeps. Big words! Over there Hans lies with the fever. And downstairs in her room – Elsa, the new maid, black boils on her face, on her hands, falls over, groaning, whimpering – alone.

"The deaf-mute, Teresa, also has a fever. And Elsa is getting worse."

"So pray with them."

Luther pours oil into his lamp. "You can go. It is not a sin to flee the plague. Take little Hans and go to Torgau. The Elector has promised us refuge and support. You can rely on it." Silently Katie stands up. She looks to the child again. He sleeps, breathing quietly. Then she begins to walk in the darkness over the creaking floor to the bedroom. But in front of her feet a shadow runs by, squeaking softly. She screams and stumbles down the steps to Wolf's bed. He is fast asleep. Katie shakes his shoulder and screams at him: "Rats! Get up! There are rats upstairs!"

Toward morning, she awakes from uneasy dreams. Luther lies beside her. He groans! He flings his arms wildly about him. She bends over him.

"Martin! Listen!" Under the influence of her talking, he slowly quietens down and continues to sleep. But she stays awake and listens.

"It is not a sin, Katie," she hears him saying.

In the morning, Greta comes out of the kitchen, her face pale.

"Elsa has died."

"Convey her quickly into the plague house! Burn her things! And fumigate!" Katie breathes heavily. She sees Wolf going across the yard with a sack. Doktor Augustin comes to see Theresa. The little girl whimpers.

"You should pray, Katie, pray," says Luther. The first pig has trouble keeping its balance, then lays down and dies. The same with the second. In the garden, the rats scurry about.

The next day, Doktor Augustin comes over with his wife. Hanna's hand clings tightly to the arm of her husband. Her face is red. She does not dare open her eyes.

"The houses around us are all empty. I cannot leave her alone when I go to visit the sick." He bites his lip. "You have empty rooms, don't you, Frau Doktor?" Katie leads the sick woman to an empty room. The floor boards are scrubbed clean. She shakes up the bed and lays fresh linen on it. "Bring her something to drink! I have to carry on. Do you also have a place for me to sleep tonight?" Katie calls Greta out of the kitchen. Together they also prepare a bed for the doctor. He comes back late, sits up for a while with Luther beside his writing desk – and then Katie hears him go to his wife. She hardly sleeps that night.

Finally it becomes cooler. The wind blows the stench away but the dying continues. The Elector sends another messenger. Shaking his head, he goes away again. No. Luther is staying and his wife also. On the hearth, Katie has a brew boiling. Daily, she pours from its contents and gives everyone some of it to drink. In the morning she searches for herbs. She does not permit Greta to help her. She weighs the herbs carefully, pulverizes them, cooks and strains them. Doktor Augustin gives her instructions in a soft voice. She nods and goes to his wife. Little Hans cries but he has to drink the brew as well. Katie takes him on her lap and gives him one spoonful after the other. Aunt Lena comes back from the market. There is not much to buy anymore.

"Have you seen anyone from the Cranach house?"

"No. But I hear that three maids have died at Reichenbachs."

Katie finds walking more and more difficult. The midwife comes by. "It looks bad. There is not a single house where someone has not died." As she sits in the evening with Luther, Katie talks about the pumpkins getting ripe. They are larger than last year. Or, about the pure water which is coming into the well which

Luther himself had dug. Clean water! His pen scratches over the paper. She watches him.

"When you were so sick in July, Doktor, and finally became well again, I thanked God with my whole heart. I thought, how good He is to us. But why does he now send us the plague?" Luther laughs.

"Why do you think so small, Katie? As though God does not know better than we, how things should go. And my sickness was worse for me than the plague. It was more of a sickness of the soul than of the body. For the devil sat on my chest so that I could hardly breathe! I would rather get black boils and go to my heavenly Father than to be tortured with healthy skin by the devil as was the case in summer."

The deaf-mute Theresa dies. The grave diggers carry her out. The basement is fumigated again. At night Katie listens. But there is no further movement between the floor boards. She becomes tired. Aunt Lena and Greta cook soup. The one task she does herself is to go to the brewery to draw out Luther's daily beer. Wolf helps her stir the vat, and dips and strains the beer.

At last, the frost comes. The plague is over. On the street, Katie again hears wagons rattling. Laughter and screaming. The students come back. Little Hans crawls around under Luther's writing table and tears off a couple of book covers. One day a messenger stands at the door. Cranach's are inviting them for a drink! Heaving a big sigh, Luther pushes his paper aside and looks at Katie with a smile:

"We made it!"

———————————

A week later, the midwife is called. Things are moving quickly. Luther is still at his lectures. Katie follows the instructions of the other women, while Aunt Lena holds her hand. The birth occurs faster than the first time. As Luther rushes up the stairs, Katie is already holding their little girl in her arms. He bends over her bed and smiles:

"Welcome – Elisabeth."[51] His face is bloated. His eyes are red. He breathes heavily ... Sighing, Katie lays back on the fresh linen sheets which Greta had prepared. She has become weak and yet she must be strong.

The house is full of guests, the world full of enemies. In innumerable papers, the man of Wittenberg is being reviled. He is said to look like the devil, his wife like a prostitute. And no matter how much Luther's friends write and how quickly the Cranach printing press gets out its tracts, they have a difficult time keeping up with the documents which revile him.

Aunt Lena comes and sits by Katie's bed. She nods encouragingly to her. Katie closes her eyes.

"If he would only accept more money ... or indeed something for his writings. Everything is given without cost, everything. But no one gives me anything free. They want to eat. He does too. Yes, he is moderate; he only wants herring. But he needs his beer. And the others, the guests, I should feed well. He is certainly a good man, Aunt Lena, but ... "

---

The cherries are ripe and the pear tree in the yard is hanging full of fruit. In the evening, the students who live in the house sit together under the trees and laugh with one another. But inside everything is quiet. Katie sits by the bed of their dead child.[52] She slips a lily from the garden under the tiny hands of the little girl. Hans brings a bouquet of flowers from the meadow and lays it on the little bed. Frightened, he holds tightly to his aunt's hand. Then Katie is alone again. She hears how Luther wanders restlessly through the rooms, up and down the steps. At last, it is quiet. After a while Katie gets up and goes up to his study. He is sitting at his writing table over a letter. Everything else he has pushed aside: his notes for a translation of the Psalms, his polemical writings, the woodcuts from Cranach.

*"Defuncta est mihi filiola mea Elisabethula ... "* "My little daughter Elisabeth has died ... My heart is sick and has become effeminate, so moved am I with misery over her. I would never have believed before that a father's heart could be so affectionate toward his children."

Katie reads the letter. She sits down at her place by the spinning wheel and stares silently in front of her at the floor. Luther's pen scratches for a little while across the paper. Then he casts it aside and gets up.

"Katie, come here! We have laughed together. Let us also weep together. The Lord will forgive me." And he takes her sobbing into his arms.

# Wittenberg, May 15, 1530

"My dear Doktor Martin Luther, sitting high up in the Colburg Castle.[53]

Dear Doktor. I received your letter. The entire household, including the students, maids and children, gathered as we read it aloud. Our little Hans sat on my lap and whispered in my ear, 'When is our dear father coming back?' I said to the child, 'My dear son, our dear father is staying away a long time but he has already written letters to us and will certainly also write you a letter if I greet him from you.' 'Yes,' he said and began to cry, 'greet him from me.' So I ask, Herr Doktor, that you also write a letter to your little son for he needs your admonition to pray properly. My dear Aunt Lena takes him on her lap each morning and evening, folds his little hands and speaks the morning and evening blessing as you have taught us. But he is as yet unable to understand it and only copies it while he looks around the room, and at little Lena[54] sitting on the floor.

The little child is thriving. It is too bad that you cannot see her. She is already a year old and I have had her portrait painted so that you do not forget your little daughter, Lena. She has big bright eyes, which beam whenever she sees a person and she seldom complains or cries. When she sees little Hans, she rejoices aloud. No one in the house can take their eyes off her, so joyfully does she laugh. I will, however, wean the child soon. I am too tied down this way. There is right now a lot of work to be done in the garden where everything is growing and blooming. If our Lord God gives His blessing, we will have a good harvest. The cherries are blooming this year in all their splendour. I can hardly wait to put some on the children's plates. The pears are not quite as good; hail destroyed many of the blossoms but if we get lots of sunshine now, there should still be a good harvest.

Our lodgers are generally satisfied. They grumble sometimes that the soup is too thin or the porridge too thick. They sometimes also want to haggle over the price of their room. The last one to do that was Jacob from Halle, whom you helped so much with your teaching. He thought I was asking too much and said that a person could lodge cheaper in Leipzig. When I told him he should go to Leipzig and seek a Doktor Martin Luther there, he only laughed. If only something good would come out of the Imperial Diet and you could return to us again. There are a number of things which I would like to talk over with you. I would really like to have another garden. What I presently harvest is not enough to fill all the hungry stomachs, especially since the orphans of your second late sister are living with us. A pair of apple trees, from whose fruit I could make puree, a garden plot to plant peas and beans, and a pond for raising fish would make me very happy. A piece of land is also being offered for sale not far from the Elster Gate near the oak grove. I have inspected it. It is a short distance to the left after the grave of our child Elisabeth. Good soil, black and fertile, no sand which the wind would immediately blow away. But I know already that you will not want to hear of it because it will cost money. But, what use are the silver goblets in the cupboard to us, which you are only keeping to give away, if I don't have the right ingredients for the soup?

Have you received your glasses? Meister Christianus wanted to send them to you in Coburg. He made a big fuss about it. I would have loved to send you some of our good beer but the messenger would not take anything except the letters and the small picture.

Wolf sends his greetings. He is not pleased that he has to work alone with me. I don't let him rest, he says. At the same time, he just takes his time, as you know. Your nephews Hans and George help him a lot but they also annoy him and use rough language so that he scolds and grumbles and has told them they should go to the devil where their parents already are. I have forbidden him to use such language but we must be more strict with the children of your late sister so that they do not bring conflict into our house and that little Hans doesn't perhaps learn bad things from them.

Hieronymus Weller is helping me faithfully with all of the daily business matters but he is a better teacher than a manager. For he can speak Latin and Greek very well but he cannot speak German so the women in the market can understand him. He has now begun to teach little Hans the beginning of the alphabet but Hans doesn't seem to understand. It appears to me that he is still too young. I had to begin to nurse little Lena again; she still seems to need breast milk.

Greet all the friends and also our nephew Cyriakus. It is good that he is a capable young man who can help you. Let me know if you have pain passing your water or if your stomach is hard as it often is. I can quickly mix something up and send it. Doktor Augustinus also asks about your health. So you see what great concern we always have about you. You can be confident that everything is well taken care of in your home and that your children and others in the house impatiently await your return. Especially, do I await your return, Herr Doktor.

Your wife in Wittenberg, May 15, 1530, after sunset.

# Wittenberg 1534-1540

Relieved, Katie pauses at the bottom of the stairs. In her arms she carries the clean fresh linen which she wants to put on the students' beds. But as she looks up the stairs to the upper floor, she hesitates. Were these stairs always this steep? Was she not always been able to hurry up the stairs without having to touch the bannisters so that when the boards creaked, everyone upstairs knew who was coming? Out of every corner of the large house come loud noises. In the basement the tradesmen are working, putting up a wall to close off the wine cellar from the barrels of herring and installing new tubs for the pickled cucumbers and cabbage. Squealing children are running through the entrance hall. Little Paul[55] is screaming. Normally one of the girls always carries him around. Martin[56] has undoubtedly gone into the garden with Melanchthon's children; they could be heard outside banging and whistling. Melanchthon's sophisticated mother probably spent money again for toys – and afterward they will say that Luther's children have broken them ...Where is little Lena? Undoubtedly with her beloved brother, who is supposed to be working but allows himself to be distracted so easily, especially when the older cousins are playing around, pushing his Latin books back and forth.

Katie pulls herself together. It should be getting warmer soon! Perhaps she misses the sun. This incessant grey sky over the flat landscape; this fog over the river every morning. In Lippendorf, it was nicer; even in Nimschen where you could see over to the thick forest. She sighs. The garden should be dug over again but as long as all the workers are busy in the basement, she can't find anyone to do it. And who will prune the roses? That is something the good Doktor does not entrust to anyone else. If possible, he still climbs out of his study into the garden himself. Oh, roses – lettuce is what she needs, and beans and turnips. You can't satisfy your hunger on roses. This year there should also be melons again. She will see to it that they don't rot like last summer. And she rejoices over the fish which grow in the pond near the meat market. Let the good Doktor tease her about her concern for trout and carp. When he has them on his plate, he will be amazed – he and the entire group which eats at the table. With this thought she feels better. She would love to have fried fish on her plate. Today, however it is too early. She will have to go out tomorrow and see about it. And on the way to the meat market she will have to pay a visit to the tailor's; he still doesn't have the garment ready for little Martin. Besides this, she needs a new large bowl. She will take care of it herself; if she sends Wolf, he will again bring a damaged piece that no one else wanted. Yesterday a small milk jug also broke and little Lena broke off the handle her cup – how that child cried!

Half way up the stairs, she has to stop again. Her head feels very hot and her heart is beating rapidly. She can hardly hold the linen in her arm. Yes, in the northwestern corner of the garden, right by the wall, where the sun is already warm in the early morning, she will prepare a new garden plot and sow some peas. Doktor Luther must write to Nurenberg again. She needs seeds anyway. And the Saxon seeds aren't any good. Let's hope the goats don't get into the garden and eat up the young shoots like last year. The gate must remain locked. Wolf must install a bolt. The children will just have to play in the yard, that's all there is to it. There is enough space there. As long as one of them doesn't walk out in front of a wagon. The bigger ones will have to watch out better. But who was watching when Martin almost wandered under the horse of the electoral messenger? How shocked she was when she heard his yelling from the kitchen! And she knew immediately that it was Martin and no one else. There could be twenty children in the monastery and a mother would know precisely who was crying.

People are continually amazed when they want to visit the esteemed Doktor Luther and eleven or twelve children rush toward them. But who is able to tame this hoard? Only when the Doktor himself appears is there silence! Then they are good and look up to him and say, Dear father – but as soon as he is out of the door ...

Katie smiles to herself. But she is still not at the top. Have the stairs become longer? From behind her she hears steps. Good morning, Frau Doktor, and with large steps, Hans Honold from Augsburg passes her. He is a spoiled young man from a wealthy home who carps sometimes about the food but learns well, according to the Doktor. And the Frau Doktor puts clean sheets on his bed. Greta should be doing it or Marie or ... But Greta is busy in the kitchen and the new maid, whom they just took in – who supposedly was a nun – has not found her feet yet. She seems to think that once she is in the house of Luther, she no longer needs to work. We do more work here than in the cloister. Elsa and Lena, the two orphans, have to help. If they want to marry well, they have to learn to do housework.

Katie's thoughts stall. Her knees are so wobbly. This is the first time she has experienced this. Or is it? Her head is hot again ... Help! Three students scramble out of their room. Shocked, one tosses aside his feathered hat and hurries down the couple of steps which Katie still needs to take to get to the top. She has slumped on the stairs. Help! The young men in their colourful jackets stand beside the unconscious woman not knowing what to do. With difficulty, they prevent her from falling down the stairs. Finally someone hears them. Aunt Lena comes panting up to them. Greta comes out of the kitchen with a towel in her hand. Guests, maids, even Wolf limps around the corner. Frau Doktor, what is wrong?

Only Luther has not heard anything. He sits at his writing table and writes a letter to the Prince of Anhalt ...Then they call him, "Doktor, your wife has collapsed on the stairs!"

"I'm fine now, Aunt Lena." Katie permits Greta and Marie to lead her to a chair. She takes a deep breath.

"Leave me alone."

Luther throws open the door.

"What is the matter?" He still has the letter in his hand. "Katie, I just wanted to tell you ... "

"Doktor, she is not well," Aunt Lena says softly to him. "She must rest now."

"No, no. I am better already." Katie tries to get up. Not knowing what to do, Luther looks from one to the other.

"Katie, I must go to Dessau. Can you get everything ready for me; above all, that good juniper juice, enough so that if the devil torments me again with my old suffering?" Aunt Lena puts her small hand on Luther's wide shoulders and gently pushes him out. But before she can close the door, little Hans rushes in, crying loudly.

"Mother ...Mother ...Don't be sick!"

"No, little Hans. No, I am feeling better already."

Katie almost succeeds in standing up. Downstairs, Paul is crying. "Bring him to me!" Elsa carries the child in and stands shyly in the corner. Elsa, put him on the floor so that he learns to walk. As Paul stands on his sturdy legs, he shouts for joy and walks towards his mother. Katie bends down and smiles as she takes him up in her arms. "Well done, my little son. Well done, my child. You are so big already. Soon there will be another little one in the house of the Doktor." Only the child can hear her soft words. But little Paul is not listening. He is entirely engrossed in feeling the bright embroidery on his mother's bodice with his fingers.

---

The east wind howls around the corners of the Black Monastery. It whistles through the cracks of the windows covered with skins. It shakes the doors and blows along the walls into town. On the streets, it is as quiet as death. Katie lies shivering in her bed. Luther in his big brown coat, his collar turned up, walks up and down. Otherwise, no one is in the house.

"I hope they make the water in the basin warm enough so that the baby doesn't catch cold."

"Now, don't worry, Katie. She will be a tough little girl if she risks coming into the world in such cold weather." [57]

He coughs. Katie straightens up.

"Go into the kitchen to the fire, Martinus! Oh, if we only had an oven, a room in which we could warm ourselves"

"... You don't have to worry about me," growls Luther. "And if God calls me to Himself, I will gladly follow. I have done my work. The Holy Scriptures have been published. Everyone can read them. Even if they don't understand. I have done what was necessary!"

"And you would leave me alone with the children?"

Shocked, Luther stands still.

"Forgive me, Katie, you are right. If God has now granted us another little daughter, we have to assume responsibility to raise her and protect her. And to build an oven where she can warm herself, but where, pray, will I get the money? In summer you want a garden and in winter you want a room with an oven. Am I a prince, a count, a robber, or a bishop, who squeezes the last penny out of his subjects? Money, always money!S Through the window they hear the bells of St. Mary's Church. It is a lonely sound in the silent town. "Not even the godparents could come," scolded Luther.

"I do hope they have warmed the water," whispers Katie.

"We can use the financial gift of the duke to make an extra room, so that the child will have an oven."

"Not only the child. Also the father – and the other children," says Katie.

Luther stands at the window and then turns to her.

"You are a brave woman. I believe that we have also now done enough in the way of filling the earth: three sturdy boys, two fine girls. I think, Katie, from now on we will live together differently."

The sound of the bells fades away. Katie folds her hands to pray for her child. Then she falls asleep.

———————————

Katie lets bread and lard be passed around. Several of the people at the table take only a little and then look expectantly over toward the kitchen from which inviting smells drift. At last Greta comes out with a flushed face and holding a steaming pot of soup. Silently everyone fills his plate. The spoons clatter. Their faces become flushed. Satisfied, Katie looks around the table. They are enjoying it. The pleasant silence is broken only by the laughing and squealing of the children as they eat in the kitchen. Dorothea, the new cook, mutters among them when the little ones make too much noise. Little Hans is already allowed to sit with the grownups. He clings tightly to his teacher, Hieronymus. He keeps his eyes down and only seldom looks out of the corner of his eye at his father who sits enthroned at the head of the large table.

Finally, Luther sets his cup down noisily, licks his lips and closes the lid of his pewter cup with a small motion of his index finger. His friends look at him. The students hold their breath. Several of them reach for their writing implements.

"What is new, sirs?" A sigh of relief is heard around the circle. Katie replenishes the soup and stirs it well so that everyone gets some of the meat. She waits eagerly to see who will begin the conversation. Hieronymus Weller clears his throat:

"Doktor, could you explain to us again why, since good works are of no benefit, you spoke so sharply against Agricola who said that one should no longer preach on good works?"[58] Katie sighs silently. Why did they have to discuss this topic today, just when she was serving such a delicious pork roast? Soon everyone will lay aside their forks and listen with open mouths while the Doktor explains again why good works are necessary and yet do not merit anything; and at the end the master of the house will become so excited that he will go without any of the good food.

Katie does not get any further in her thoughts. Their niece Elsa emerges in the doorway and signals excitedly to her. Katie waves for her to come in.

"And so it's right to preach as I did to the princes that they should do their duty and carry out good works for the benefit of all of us but we should still not think that our Father in heaven ..." Luther thunders at his hearers. Katie listens to the soft whispering of the girl:

"Please come, Frau Doktor. Aunt Lena is not well." As quickly as she can, Katie follows the child who races in front of her up the stairs. She cannot quite keep up and reaches the door of Aunt Lena's room quite out of breath. The old woman is sitting in an armchair by the open window, her head leaning back, her forehead flushed.

"Aunt Lena!" A brief dry cough shakes the thin body of the sick woman. "We must call Doktor Augustin! Elsa, run. Let Wolf know! And also the Doktor!"

She sits down beside the sick woman and strokes her hand. Anxiously she looks at her gaunt face. After a while, Magdalena von Bora opens her eyes.

"Katie?"

"Yes, Aunt Lena?"

"Why are you weeping, child? It is time. I am thirsty ..." She struggles for breath. Katie goes out calling and scolding until at last someone brings a jug of beer. Later the doctor comes. He rubs the chest of the sick woman and shrugs his shoulders. Magdalena wants to speak but isn't able to do so.

By the time Luther comes to the room, it is already dusk outside. After the meal where he had discussed the ten commandments with his friends at the table, he had forgotten the message. Now he stands hesitatingly in the doorway. The sick woman moans. With a loud voice, he addresses her,

"Aunt Lena. Listen. You will see the morning star arise in the Kingdom of God! What an awakening that will be!" She does not answer. The door opens again. A young woman in a well-worn velvet garment stands in the room.

"Her Royal Highness, the Elector's wife, asks for the Frau Doktor." Katie rings her hands. Of course! She was supposed to go to see the sick Elector's wife after the meal. The old lady wouldn't eat unless Katie sat by her bed. "Elsa, stay here with Aunt Lena, but call me if ..."

She walks past the young lady-in-waiting, whose train rustles over the floorboards, and goes down the stairs into the apartments which had been hastily outfitted for their royal guest. Elisabeth von

Brandenburg lifts her gaunt head as Katie comes in. Her food is untouched beside her bed. Her long fingers with their expensive rings lie over the edge of the bed. Spit runs from her mouth. Katie takes a cloth and wipes it off.

"She has again not eaten anything," complains the servant. Silently, Katie takes the spoon.

"Sit her up", she orders curtly. Listlessly, the Elector's wife allows herself to be propped up. Katie strokes her hand soothingly.

"Your Highness, please have some of my soup." As with a small child, she spoons some soup into the mouth of the woman, followed by some bread and places the jug of wine to her mouth. She has water brought and washes the sick woman. Then she returns to Aunt Lena.

Night comes. After a while it is quiet in the house. From the garden and the river bank, Katie hears the night animals calling. Again and again the sick woman tosses about with fits of coughing. Katie holds her hand, wipes the sweat from her forehead, and spoons some herbal drink into her mouth. Toward morning, both of them sink into a brief uneasy sleep.

As the sun comes up and the cock triumphantly announces the new day, Katie wakes with a start. Aunt Lena is not moving. Although she is breathing weakly, she does not seem to have any more pain. Suddenly however, she rises, struggling for breath. Her struggle lasts a long time. Katie screams in despair but no one hears. At last the sick woman falls back on her bed and is still. Her limbs slowly relax. Her breathing is irregular, not recognizable any more.[59]

Katie stares at her face, illumined by the first rays of the sun. After a while she stands up and closes the eyelids of the dead woman. "*Requiem aeternam dona eis ...* " Grant them, Lord, eternal rest and may the everlasting light shine upon them. As the old, almost forgotten words pass her lips, it is as if the door to the inner convent garden opens and a white nun comes out into the cold night, gives her a jug of hot infusion for a sick child and vanishes again into the darkness.

"Aunt Lena!" Her tears fall on the garment of the dead woman where they form small spots.

The Black Monastery awakens noisily. Katie pulls her skirt into place and ties her bonnet tightly. She hears the children calling. Soon after, a messenger rides into the courtyard. Through the window, Katie sees Luther walk out to him. He holds a letter in his hands. She goes down slowly and meets Luther in the courtyard. Aunt Lena has died. Luther is reading. He raises his head and looks at her.

"She is with our Father in heaven, Katie. I wish we were there too." He reads on. Katie goes back into the house. In the kitchen, she weeps with the children-until Luther comes in.

"We must give the messenger some food and drink," says Luther.

"Where is he from?"

"From the Princess of Anhalt. She wants to visit her mother."

Katie puts down the knife with which she had begun to cut off a piece of bread. "No, Doktor. No!" Her voice becomes loud and piercing.

"She writes that she will come with a small entourage. Katie, we can't offend the princess."

"We can't do it, Doktor. We don't have a free room in the entire monastery. Where would you have the princess sleep? Should we put her up in the stable? And her entourage in the pig sty? Should I throw out the students or your books, Doktor? Out of pity for the aging wife of the Elector and because she remained faithful to the true doctrine, I took her in and cared for her as if she was my own mother. And I have also had to feed her entourage who turned up their noses at my soup and my roast because they wanted something better in their courtly bellies than we and our children have. But now the grand dame, the daughter – no, Doktor. That I will not do."

Crying, Paul and Margaret cling to the skirt of their mother. Martin creeps under the table. Luther stands helplessly in the middle of the kitchen and looks around.

"Where is Aunt Lena?" All of a sudden everything becomes quiet. Katie sobs into her hands.

"Right. It's all right, Katie." He rolls up the document. "I will answer that it is not convenient. Stop crying, Katie. Give the messenger a jug of beer. But be quiet. And you children too. This wailing is unbearable." He shoos the children out of the kitchen, strokes Katie's shoulders helplessly, and then goes to his study with heavy steps.

"With the churchyard being so close to the market, even the dead don't find rest anymore," says Luther. "Worse things are happening there than in the courtyard of Herod's temple." So they bury Magdalena von Bora in the new cemetery by the Elster Gate, not far from Elizabeth.

---

A few days later, with Margaret holding onto her hand, Katie goes through town to the pig market. Tolpel runs barking at her side. Katie is lost in thought. Barbara Cranach joins up with her not far from the church.

"So, Frau Doktor, have you become proud?"

"Barbara!" The wife of the rich painter who is the present mayor is as always magnificently dressed. Two maids walk beside her carrying her basket filled with materials. But the face of the proud woman is pale.

Katie puts down her basket and stretches her arms out to Barbara.

"How are things going with you, Barbara?" she asks softly. With a regal wave of her hand, Barbara sends her maids to the Cranach house.

"Since the report came from Bologna," She can barely go on and buries her face in her scarf. "I can't sleep anymore, Katie. I always dream about it ... I see him lying in the straw somewhere, in some dreadful place. My son! And the Meister ... He walks about in the house, every night. He calls: 'Hans! Hans!' As though he could call the young man back to life. He rails against God."

Margaret and Tolpel romp around between the skirts of the two women. The little girl laughs. The dog yaps. "Don't scream like that, Maruschel," [60] Katie interrupts.

"He will never get over his firstborn's being taken from him," says Barbara.

"You can't hold on to them." In the high tower of the church, the noon bell begins to peel. A fully loaded farm wagon clatters past close to the women. Tolpel is almost caught under its wheels. In the noise, they part in silence.

As they arrive at the garden near the pig market, Katie looks first at the fish in the pond. The carp have become nice and fat. "Here," exclaims Maruschel joyfully. But she is not referring to the fish. In the mirror of the deep water, Margaret has recognized her own laughing reflection. Katie bends down over the little girl and holds her tightly with both her arms. Behind the mirror image of the child emerges the face of an older woman, broad and solid, with deep creases above her nose, a deep indented dimple in her chin, large dark eyes and full eyebrows. The corners of the kerchief tied over her head are evident on the right and left. Small ripples pass through her smile and lose themselves in the reflection of the sky.

---

Katie sits by the window in the warm room. Through the bottle glass window a little light still falls on her hands. Nearby Maruschel crawls around on the seat of the cupboard and runs her finger carefully over the glass.

"Nice!" She looks at her mother and laughs. Katie smiles back,

"Yes, nice – and expensive. Your father didn't want to pay it. But now the cold wind stays outside.

"And we can sing a nice year," croons Maruschel.

"The word is new year, child; but it is not even Christmas yet."

"Oh but soon, Mother! Greta told me it will soon be Christmas." Katie studies Martin's torn jacket and wonders which fence he has crawled over. Just as well his father has not seen it!

She hears a noise downstairs. Heavy steps approach through the anteroom. Luther's penetrating voice rises above the creaking of the floorboards. With a jerk, the door is torn open. Cold air streams in.

"Here they are!" Luther shoves four thin children ahead of him, three boys and one girl. Fearful, the smallest boy clings tightly to the hand of his sister. The older ones stand stiffly and upright and stare at the strange woman. "Children, this is the Domina," says Luther. Katie lays the jacket aside, stands up and straightens out her dress with her hands. Maruschel also scrambles down from her seat by the window and approaches the new arrivals in amazement.

"Katie, dear Lord Katie, I know ..."

"Did you not say there were two children? Whether it is two or four ..." Katie strokes the head of the little girl with her hand. She looks up shyly, her mouth half open. Her hands are shaking. "Barbara was outraged when I related to her what you had in mind," says Katie. "There will be a rebellion in Wittenberg. They will say that we are allowing the plague to come into town."

Luther clenches his fist.

"They allow their own children to starve! It is as if there is no more love among people. I tell you, Katie, more people died from fright during the plague than from the plague itself!"

"Yes, Doktor Luther. You may be right. Except it doesn't do the orphans any good!" She looks at him sternly. Surely he must know that she would not send a child away – even if it carried the plague. "Come," she says and takes the hand of the little boy. "We will stick you into the bath tub where Greta can give you a good scrubbing. Then go into the kitchen and get something to eat. And then I will show you your room."

That evening as Luther lay down beside her, he says, "Katie, forgive me!"

"For what should I forgive you, Herr Luther?

"I thought … As I heard that the professor and his wife had left four children … I was afraid."

"Why were you afraid, Martinus? Were you afraid that your wife would abandon them to their fate? Did you think that?"

"No, Katie. But I was afraid, that you … "

"If I only had an estate, a decent piece of land."

"Katie, you already have so many garden plots!"

"Yes, garden plots, small gardens. I turn around once and everything is harvested. A piece of land, Martin: fields, decent fields across which the wind can blow. And horses to cultivate them. You have always lived behind walls."

"Katie, you are extravagant. You already have a whole monastery."

"Yes, a monastery full of hungry bellies. We have just added four children, Martinus! And—and soon ... another one of our own."

"No, Katie!" Luther sat upright in bed. "I did not want that! Oh, my sinful flesh ... Oh, wretched man that I am!"

"What are you saying, sinful flesh. I am your wife. I am not too old to bring a child into this world. Many women have had healthy children at forty."

Groaning, Luther sinks back down again.

"But I should have exercised moderation as I preach it to others. I am an old man and death was staring me in the face. You know I bade you farewell and would have been content ..."

"But God has reawakened you to life, Herr Doktor. This has been a delight to me and to the children. Just think how old Abraham was."

"Yes, Katie, you know your Bible when it comes to contradicting me. Woe is me for permitting women to read the Holy Scriptures. And yet Katie, it was not right of me to follow the example of Abraham. But our child shall not pay for that. We will accept it thankfully just as we did all the others. So, go to sleep, Katie, and pray that Satan will spare me tonight! By day it is people and at night the devil – how can a soul bear it? Oh, my Lord Jesus Christ!"

He blows out the candle, the bed creaks as he turns over, and soon he is breathing deeply and quietly. Katie lays awake and thinks: *Much as we would like to do it, we cannot squeeze any more pigs into the sty.*

———————

A fever rolls over Katie's body in hot waves. Her head pulses with pain. As if through a wall of fog, she hears

Doktor Augustin scold: "Is no one bringing me fresh towels? I need hot water! Move! A basin!"

The doors bangs. Someone runs hurriedly up and down the stairs. Pain tears her innards, ebbing and waning. She screams.

"No!"

Someone strokes her hand and cools her forehead. She whimpers. Then she loses consciousness.

When she comes to again, her pain has abated. But she is unable to move. The room is quiet. The doors are wide open so that some heat from the living room can come into the bedroom. From the small window, freezing air blows in. Luther is kneeling at her bed. He has buried his head so deeply in the straw mattress that she recognizes only the dark locks which fall to the nape of his powerful neck. Weakly, she stretches out her hand for him. He gives a start.

"Katie, Katie, don't die on me! Katie, it is my fault!" She hears him sobbing like a little child.

Her hand is too weak and falls. He grabs it and presses it to his mouth. Outside, the sound of the children can be heard. For a moment, Katie is completely awake.

"How are the children?" Luther gives a start.

"Katie, speak! Speak again! Katie, you will get better again. Yes, yes, the children are fine. But they need you. We all need you. Lenschen," [61] he calls toward the hall. A small girl appears at the door. "Lenschen, your mother has spoken! Go and tell Doktor Augustin! Go to the kitchen! Tell Dorothea to make a bit of soup." Madgelena hugs her father and darts out. A few moments later she returns with a mug.

"Try it," says Luther and steps back from the bed. He straightens up, pushes his unruly hair from his face and observes as Lenschen gently and patiently gives her mother tiny quantities of the liquid.

The floorboards in the sitting room creak. Everyone speaks in hushed tones. Luther proceeds to the sitting room. Jonas and Melanchthon sit at a table and look at him expectantly. Their friend Bugenhagen comes into the room, snow still on his cap.

"She spoke. Lenschen is giving her milk."

"Thank God!"

The friends absentmindedly turn pages in the books which are lying in front of them on the oak table. After a while Lenschen comes from the bedroom. She shows them the mug. Her mother had consumed some of its contents.

"I think she is sleeping."

"Good girl!" Luther pulls the girl on to his lap and holds her close. Several of the boarders appear in the doorway and look questioningly at the master of the house. He waves them away. His friends also pack up their papers. "Tomorrow," says Luther, "we will continue. Is the prophet Jeremiah saying, 'They will come crying, but I will comfort and lead them'? Should we use the word 'lead', gentlemen, or guide? Or does the prophet perhaps rather mean protect? What does the Hebrew text say? Or does it say 'heal'? Tomorrow we will discuss this. That's all for today, thank you." Silently, the men go out. On the steps, they continue in whispers to consider the question.

Lenschen sits down again on the bed of the sick woman. The other children crowd around their father who stares darkly into space.

"Father, shall I bring your lute?" Paul asks.

Amazed, Luther looks up. "Yes, my son, you are right. We will sing Satan out of the house. And your mother will hear it and stay with us! Where is my lute? Where is our hymnal? Come, let us sing!" Hesitantly at first, than more and more bravely, the children begin to sing. Katie opens her eyes.

"And if my pain lasts till the night
and comes again in morning light;
 My heart shall neither doubt nor care
 for God with might is surely there. "

"Do you feel better, mother?" Lenschen asks anxiously. Katie sighs softly. Then she falls into a light sleep.

———————————

The pear tree in the courtyard is in blossom. The boarders are stretched out on the ground. The children sit around in a circle. Even Luther has left his study and is walking up and down, deep in thought with Melanchthon. Katie sits on a stool among the others and hems a table cloth. Occasionally she looks over at the two men. Their expressions are so serious that even the long-time boarders do not dare to speak to them. The grown-ups know what they are discussing: the secret advice which Luther had given regarding the bigamy of the Landgrave Philipp of Hesse[62] – so secret was it that the sparrows on the roofs sang it out![63] Luther permitted it and children would ask their mothers: what does it mean to have a 'marriage on the left hand'?[64]

While Melanchthon reflects with a bowed head and walks to and fro, Luther speaks loudly and gesticulates fiercely: "The illicit sexual relationships of the archbishop who is having an affair with ten women at the same time, they let pass as a venial sin but he wanted to act honourably toward the young woman. "

The students smirk.

Katie is also restless. A messenger came yesterday to announce an unexpected visitor. She looks over at Luther. How will he receive the brother-in-law whom he has never met? How will her brother act toward her? She didn't even know what he looked like any more. Would he look like their father? Would he still be so arrogant? Will he curse and ridicule the clergymen as many people in his social standing were prone to do? The sun is already setting in the west. It is time to eat. Katie gets up and waves to the hungry boarders. She feels friendly towards them today. Her generosity towards her household makes her proud. Her noble brother can come and see.

He does not arrive until evening. For a long time Luther has been sitting with his friends in his study. They follow the thought of Jeremiah, searching for the correct German word for his lament and comfort, when Hans von Bora rides into the courtyard. Katie walks toward him.

"So, my sister, I did not think I would find you in such circumstances."

"I am happy to see you, Herr von Bora."

"Frau Doktor was so good as to write to me even though it was not me who helped you out of the monastery."

"I don't carry a grudge. How are things going with you and your family?"

"Not very well. Thank you for asking. We are short of everything except children. But I see that you also have them in abundance."

"We thank God for them."

"That attitude befits you as a convent woman. I cannot help you with money. I only thought – perhaps you might want to buy a piece of the traditional family estate. I came to offer you the property of Zuelsdorf. It is the last piece of land from the von Bora estate which has not been spent on drink, mortgaged or sold."

"So, how did you get along with your brother," asks Luther when they were alone. Katie sits on the bed and braids her hair into a plait. She is quiet. "Was it such an ordeal? Did he offend you?"

"No," says Katie hesitantly. Then she stands up and looks squarely at him. "When I seemed to be at death's door this winter, Doktor Luther, did you not make a promise to me?"

"Did I do that? It was careless of me."

"Yes, you did. If I can find a piece of land, you said, you shall have it; Hans wants to sell the Zuelsdorf property to us."

"For how much?"

"He is asking 700 gulden but I think that he will be satisfied with 600." [65]

"I am a poor man. Where will I get that kind of money?"

"If you would only take the money for your writings which people offer you for a change; if you would earn only half as much as our friend Hans Lufft who prints them, we would not have any money worries, my dear Doktor!"

"No, Katie, you must not talk like that. But I will ask the Elector. He will help me if I tell him that my greedy wife does not let me work in peace ..." Katie laughs brightly:

"Do as you like, Martinus, but I can promise you that if I get Zuelsdorf, you will never again hear me complain – never again – never again!"

"That I believe, my dear, for then you will not be in Wittenberg very often."

# Zuelsdorf 1540-1541

The wind blows grey rain clouds across the sky. Under the falling rain the forests cower. Water drops into puddles from the canvas which covers the wagon. The wheels turn with difficulty in the mud. "Whoa!" The horses stop immediately and shake their manes. Adam, who sits on the seat of the coach, stands up and pushes back his cap. Katie, who had opened up the canvas, grabs his shoulder.

"There! Don't you see it?" Adam growls something and steers the horses somewhat to the left onto a path almost overgrown. Water fills the deep furrows in the path. Katie leans back. The rain runs over her face.

Of the gate through which they pass only one post is standing. A large lean dog runs barking toward them. Out of the barn which has no door, a woman calls it back. Before Adam is able to help her, Katie has jumped down from the wagon and is trying to find a path between the puddles to the house from whose chimney smoke is rising. In spite of the barking of the dogs, no one there seems to notice or care about their arrival. With a jolt, Katie shoves open the wooden door. The room in front of her is pitch dark. An old woman shuffles out of a corner with a flickering candle. The maid raises the light. Frightened bats fly from one end of the hall to the other. Katie folds up her coat and looks around her.

"Go ahead into the room," she commands the old woman. The light sways in front of her. A door creaks. The small hallway of the house is gloomy. The wind whistles through the boarded up windows.

Katie lays her bundle on the table and looks around. She takes the lamp from the shaky old woman and illuminates the walls. There! In the flickering light of the lamp the sad eyes of a young woman become alive. Her face remains dark. Her mouth is shaped into a forced smile.

"Mother!" The old woman begins to cackle. Katie puts down the light and continues: "Quit that, Josepha! Where are the others? Why is there no fire in the hearth? Is there anything for us to eat? Why are you not working? Do you think you can sit around just because it is raining? I want to see the livestock. My horses must be taken care of. And tomorrow morning, Adam will check to see about that leak in the roof." As she stops talking, only the rhythmic drops of water falling from the roof on the table can be heard. "I need building supplies," sighs Katie, "a large quantity of building supplies. If I only had them before winter. But then summer will come again."

---

My dearest, learned and famous Doktor Martinus in Wittenberg, together with all the boarders, children and guests. Grace and peace in Christ to you all!

We arrived here safe and sound, making the trip from Eilenburg without difficulty in one day. All of our equipment also arrived undamaged. Much has changed since last year. Our only problem is that we still do not have enough wood because we were cheated by the senior official of Altenburg. As a result, the house has been repaired but one wall of the barn is so rotten that it is in danger of collapsing in a storm. I pray, therefore, Herr Doktor, that you ask the Elector to let me know when I can again take some logs from Altenburg for I am afraid that there is still much to be done here. Also with all the mismanagement, the peasants here have become so lazy that they hardly care properly for the cattle. In addition, the local farmers are challenging our right to the pasture which has always belonged to the estate. This is what happens when there is no master to keep an eye on things. However, my heart is glad when I see the grain growing in the fields. Our dear Father in heaven has provided us sufficient rain and sunshine. But there will not be enough oats to feed the horses through the summer. Might we ask a friend to loan us some? After harvest he will get it back. I swear. I certainly sowed enough oats.

Lenschen and Maruschel, together with old Josepha, have swept and washed down the house so that it shines like a manor, properly prepared for our Doktor, should he want to turn his back on horrible Wittenberg and the fortifications of the town. It is possible that some worthwhile thoughts could come down to him from the expanse of the heavens. Here no one builds a wall in front of our house as is the case in Wittenberg. Also no woman has time to stand in the market to show off her attire. Instead the dear Lord adorns the land with His flowers.

So, everything is going well on our estate. I wish you would come, dear Doktor, to sit with me at table and eat wild game which comes from the abundant woods. The cherries will also soon be ripe. To add to this abundance, I would love to buy you a little barrel of wine from Altenburg.

I have also had the picture of my mother spruced up and have hung a picture of you and me beneath it. Our good John has carved us out of stone. The Doktor, whom he has never seen, very young; Me so old.

The girls were very pleased with it. Now everyone can see who this little estate belongs to. I have also planted a rose bush for the Doktor, which is already in bloom. I have to end now since I want to pray with the girls the evening blessing as you taught to us. My candle has also burned down already and we want to save our candles. After all, the dear Lord will let the sun shine again tomorrow early.

Tell the boys, they should study diligently and make their teachers happy. Perhaps their dear father will then also permit them to come to this little estate where they can practice speaking Latin to the cattle and horses. May God watch over you. Make sure that your dear father receives his beer each day. In a few weeks we will be with you again – with a wagon full of treasures of which many a prince would be jealous.

Written in Zuelsdorf after Trinity 1541, Katharina Lutherin

Katie snuffs out the candle, seals the letter and stands up. Outside it is already dark. When she calls the girls, no one answers. She finds her daughters in their rooms on their straw mattresses, fast asleep. Softly she creeps out again and walks across the courtyard. Ahab, the big dog, presses up against her side. After her arrival, he was the first to grasp who the boss of the house was ... Out of the stable comes the soft sound of snorting from the horses. The cattle are outside with a young herdsman on the pasture. Soon calves will be born.

In the moonlight she sees in front of her the path which leads to the restored gate and out into the fields. Not far from her to the east, the Mulde river flows by the ruined walls of the Throne of Mary convent. And somewhere to the north, two days journey, lies Wittenberg. So many roads lead through the land here and there. As a small child, she had once started out from here. And now she has come home as Lady of Zuelsdorf. She smiles.

———————————

The harvest wagon sways through the gate. Katie stands in front of the door of the house, her hands on her hips. Yes, that should be sufficient. In the barn the sacks stand ready to be loaded up for Wittenberg. The barn is repaired. Soon the cows will be brought in. Oh but the apples! Maruschel and Lenchen are behind the house in the orchard filling their baskets. The sun glows like a red ball above the woods by Altenburg. They must make haste. Old Josepha takes her broom and sweeps behind the wagon. Adam jumps from the coach seat and wipes the sweat from his eyes.

"Yes, Frau Doktor," he says, "we have done it." And he points with great pride to the two bays. "These are horses! Of them you can be proud. Give them water, Adam, brush them down. Your praise will not be sufficient to feed them."

A figure comes toward them on the dusty road. Who is that? Ahab runs barking out of the barn. The stranger is walking slowly, apparently tired.

"It's Urban! Frau Doktor, it's Urban." Katie is startled. A messenger from Wittenberg? She gathers up her dress and runs across the yard. Urban has stopped at the gate and is looking around him, not knowing where to go. When he recognizes the mistress, he feels relieved.

"Urban, what are you bringing us?"

"A letter from Doktor Luther." They walk out of the dusty heat into the kitchen. Katie's hands are shaking as she unfolds the envelope. While she does this,

Urban greedily drinks the fresh milk, wipes his mouth with the back of his hand and relates:

"That was some woman to whom you entrusted the management of your home. If it had not been for the fact that good Dorothea remained faithful, you would find few of your things remaining. Rosina von Truchsess! She was a peasant whore, not a nun. She has ..."

Katie walks to the open window and reads:

> "My dear homemaker, Frau Doktor, pig trader and Mistress of Zuelsdorf.
>
> Dear Katie, I am herewith sending Urban to you so you might not become frightened should you hear the shout of the Turks. And I am surprised that you have not written, for you certainly must know that we here would be concerned about you, given that Mainz, Heinz and many nobles in Meissen are very hostile toward us. Harvest and sell what you can and come home. It seems to me we are heading into a miry bog just as a storm is breaking; God is going to visit us with His anger, on account of our sins."

Laughing and singing, Lenchen and Maruschel come across the farmyard with their baskets full of red apples. What a day! thinks Katie. God is pouring the riches of his earth over us. But He does not allow us to enjoy them. She folds up the letter and sticks it into her apron pocket.

"Adam, we already have to load the sacks today. Josepha, bake three loaves of bread for our trip. We leave the day after tomorrow."

"So we must hurry, Mistress?"

In the meantime, Urban has made himself comfortable on the bench in front of the house beside the rose bush. Katie sits down beside him.

"Tell me more!" She takes a basket of beans and puts them into bags.

"The Doktor chased Rosina, the false nun, out of the house scolding her severely. Her story was a pack of lies. And then," Urban drops his voice and looks around smirking ... "and then she became pregnant." Katie sighs. "The Doktor stormed about in his room. And the boys did not dare leave the sitting room. It took all of the boarders to quiet him down. Then came the reports about the Turks. They are coming closer. Also the bloodhound Heinrich von Braunschweig has again made himself the topic of conversation. In any case," Urban chews on a piece of straw and shakes his head, "our Doktor was sure that the Lord would not tolerate so much malice. So he sent me to report to you, Frau Doktor."

Katie ties up a sack and wipes her hands clean on her apron. "Go into the kitchen, Urban, and have Josepha prepare you some soup. Then rest. Tomorrow we will pack up. Fortunately, the harvest has been gathered. I will leave it for Adam to market." She looks up at the sky. The birds are gathering for their flight to the south. Autumn fogs are rising over the plains. I have stayed too long, she thinks.

# Wittenberg 1542-1546

"Stop crying, Katie! She is with God. She si..g..  ...r song of praise to the heavenly father with her happy little voice and you cry! Stop it, now!". Luther lifts his voice threateningly. They are alone in the wood-panelled room. The windows stand open. The golden light of the evening sun streams outside over the gardens and ramparts beyond the Black Monastery. Katie sits at her place by the window and holds a handkerchief in front of her eyes.

"Stop it, now!"

She blows her nose and looks at him.

"Why should I stop? My child has died. Why am I not allowed to weep?" Luther stops his restless pacing and lifts his index finger.

"You should thank God like Job did. Don't you remember? The Lord has given, the Lord has taken away, blessed be the name of the Lord. Your little daughter is in good hands. Our Lenchen died like a saint. Would to God that we could be where she is! Redeemed from all evil – from the Papists, the Turks, the false friends."

"Oh, yes, I am supposed to thank God. And what about you, Herr Doktor? Did I not hear you sobbing for three nights beside me? Did you thank God that your daughter was taken away from you?"

"I know, Katie, I know. I was weak. Our flesh makes us want to hold on to what is ours. And she was so lovable and good ..."

The door is opened without a sound. Elsa, their niece, slips in, looking around cautiously herself.

"What is it?" Luther asks sternly.

"Dorothea wants me to ask how many cakes she should bake for Sunday," stutters the young girl.

"Cakes! Cakes! I don't want any cakes. I don't want any guests," sobs Katie.

"Will you stop, this instant!"

Elsa looks helplessly from one to the other.

"Tell the cook, that we will not have any guests." Luther pushes her out through the door and comes back to Katie. "Katie, Submit yourself to God's will. Submit yourself! I do it too!" Quickly he goes out of the door and she hears him give instructions outside. Then he stamps up the stairs to his study. Katie remains sitting.

In the clear sky, a flock of wild geese fly by. Their honking calls fade away on the other side of the town. Katie lifts her head and her gaze follows them. Such a small piece of sky remains for her. Out there, in Zuelsdorf, one could see so far! But now Adam is on his own again, harvesting and selling. How she would have loved to stay there and bring in the harvest! But Lenschen became ill ... She sees herself again with the feverish child rushing over the dusty road in the swaying coach, feeling the heat and the thirst and fear in her heart. She remembers the doctor shaking his head anxiously, the nights at the sickbed, the slow but constant ebbing of the child's life under her hands – and the dream. Two young men stood beside her. 'What do you want?' she had called out, startled. 'What do you want so richly adorned and radiant at the bed of my child?' 'To a wedding, we want to take her – to a wedding."

When she awoke, she had said joyfully,

"Lenchen, God does not want you to die." Full of joy, she had said to Melanchthon when he came to ask how things were going:

"Consider, Magister, what I have dreamed! Is this not a good sign?" But then – his face! At the sorrowful look of her friend, clarity suddenly came. It was not her mother who would outfit Lenchen for the wedding.

It was not her earthly father who would give his daughter to a fine husband – God was calling the little girl to a wedding ... Never again her beautiful voice in the garden, singing, laughing. Never again the soft whisper in her ear: 'Mother, I want to tell you something.' Katie allows her tears to come. Who has the right to forbid her to cry for her child?

A cool wind comes up. Out in the garden, the voices of the boys who are just coming from their lessons could be heard – Paul, Martin, the nephews and Melanchthon's sons. Instead of reading more of Augustine, they are chasing the hens through the garden plots. Katie listens.

*If Luther hears the children romping about, he will be annoyed again and threaten with his stick. Fortunately, the man is quicker with words than with actions and the beatings are almost always averted if she comes between them in time. She should get up, go into the brewery or into the pig sty where an animal is sick. But she remains seated. Lost in thought, she studies her hands. Like writing in an unknown language, protruding veins show through the backs of her hands. Is this the way God writes His will for her life?*

*With these hands she had received her child after birth. With these hands she had washed and changed her, caressed and fed her. With these hands she had bathed her fevered brow as her life touched its end.*

Tears flow from her eyes again. She thinks about Barbara, who had become proud and hard after she had lost her son – Barbara also died and Aunt Lena and little Elisabeth and now her Lenchen, only fourteen years old, still so young, so young! And Luther speaks of Job. Perhaps Job's children were older. But would that have been better for her? No, Job was a man – and not a mother. Mary, Mary on the Pietà picture in the convent church – *she* knew what it was all about!

She thinks about Hans, their oldest. His image comes to her – grown up, slender and pale, with large wide-open eyes. Hans is with his cousin Florian in Torgau – only a couple of hours away but, in spite of this, much too far. She does not know how he is faring. Yes, he has always insisted that everything was going very well in Herr Krodel's school and withFrau Krodel in the house. He could learn better there than in the Black Monastery where it buzzed and hummed as in a bee hive. But when he got back into the coach after Lenchen's funeral – did he not swallow back his tears so that no one should see them, above all his father?

*His father! While on his own account he cried and complained like a child that Satan has struck him so hard, he would not permit others to open their mouths, especially not his son – she sighs. Her glance stops at her wedding ring which she has worn for so many years. There shines the blood red ruby – in the middle of the tools of torture. Yes, it was a nun's ring, although she had married a normal human being. Inside is his name — but outside, in the finest goldsmith's work, is a picture of the crucified. Indeed every marriage is also a cross.*

She gets up, closes the window and climbs up to Luther's study. As she enters he does not look up. But he mutters, "You should thank God three times daily for your Christian husband. "

"I do that six times daily, but can you give me a good reason?"

Luther smiles to himself, "I am just now writing a recommendation to the Council in Basel that they should not forbid the publication of the Koran. Someone has made a new translation and it seems to me that there is nothing better for women to read than the Koran to see what is happening among the Turks where one man can marry four wives."

Then he tosses his quill to the side and begins to dig around and search among the stacks of books which are piled up to his right and to his left.

"Listen, I want to read to you the poem which I have written for the grave stone of our dear daughter.

Here I, Lenchen, Doktor Luther's daughter, sleep.
In my small bed I rest with all the saints in God's keep.
Like them I too was born in sin
Doomed forever with my kin
But now I live and have it well
Saved by Christ's blood from sin and hell."

Katie nods without great enthusiasm.

"Actually I wanted to write more. I wanted to write that all of us wish soon to be where she is now – but the passers-by might misunderstand."

"I think that our Father in heaven knows why he has put us on this earth. And so we should place ourselves in His will. Do you not always say that, Doktor?"

"Yes, Frau Doktor, I place myself there, perhaps at the moment even more so than you."

"You did not give birth to this child, suckle and feed her."

"No, but I also loved her."

"Then you will understand that I worry about Hans. I fear that he will become ill from homesickness. I told him that he should come home if he is not well."

"The devil you did!" Luther strikes his fist on the table so hard that the ink bottle jumped up. "At last, the boy has time and quiet to learn properly and become a man. He is fine with our friend Krodel but now you ..."

"I am telling you that I worry because he was so pale and hardly ate anything."

Luther springs to his feet. "That was during the days after Lenchen died. Who among us was eating? And naturally, he was grief stricken as all of us were. But that is no reason. No, Katie, Hans will stay in Torgau. You have mollycoddled the boy. He must finally become a man. I will not hear any more about it."

Katie pulls her handkerchief awkwardly from her pocket and wipes her eyes, while Luther storms around the room. Finally she straightens herself and says,

"Does it not say in the Holy Scriptures that fathers should love their sons? Should you not also, Herr Doktor, show the boys kindness once in a while instead of always scolding them?"

"Whoever loves his son will discipline him! You are a woman. You don't understand that."

Katie looks out of the corner of her eye over her handkerchief at Luther.

"Yes, I have noticed it. God is a stern father and you take after Him, Doktor. I can sometimes hardly believe that He would give his only son."

"Don't venture into sin, Katie! For the world, He did it; for the entire world!"

"In spite of that, I would not have done it," says Katie very softly, as she closes the door behind her.

———————

The hot day didn't seem to want to end. Katie came out of the brewery and stood in the court yard. The students and boarders, as well as the maids and nieces, stretched out in the shade of the pear trees, as if there was no work to be done in the yard and garden.

"Elsa, Anna, Margaret!" The girls jumped up. Elsa blushed. Pretty Anna looked at the ground. Only small Maruschel looked her mother mischievously in the face.

"Oh, mother, it is just too warm!"

"Off with you, into the garden! The vegetable plots need watering! Dorothea needs vegetables for tomorrow. Check if the melons are ripe yet."

"We will help you," called an impertinent young man who had just come from Nurenberg into the house – and had brought greetings from a certain Hieronymus Baumgaertner, greetings and a report which made Katie's heart beat a little too rapidly. All was not well with Hieronymus. He was in prison, the report said. A feud, a marauding, ungodly knight – Katie's thoughts wandered off into the distance, otherwise she would surely have raised an objection as not only the girls and maids but also six or seven young men ran into the garden amidst loud laughter and joking, to do the work which they had been instructed to do.

Suspiciously Katie followed them with her eyes. What was going on? She already heard the excited stirring of startled animals in the pigsty. And from the well came yelling and screaming – instead of watering the vegetables, it appeared that a water fight had broken out between the boys and the girls. How loose the morals of young people had become! Without shame, the boys looked at the girls. And from this came secret engagements, against which Doktor Luther scolded even from the pulpit, because rights and ordinances had become confused. Exhausted, Katie sank down on the stone seat beside the gate of the house. On the underside of the canopy was a rose, carved out of sandstone, Luther's rose. The place opposite her on the other side of the portal was empty. But the canopy had a picture of the man to whom the place belonged. She wished he was there with her and that she could speak to him – about Hieronymus, about the young people who ran around there in the garden, about the drought, about the talk of war, about the fact that things seemed to be completely chaotic in the world!

She sat in the shade. The sun was already setting over the town. Only a few young people were reclining in small groups under the trees in the yard. Sitting did her good. Her hands felt the cool stone. Hieronymus thirsting in a prison – and Martinus on the way. He was supposed to return one of these days from Zeitz, where he had visited his old friend Amsdorf. Travelling was exhausting for him. What would be his state of mind when he came home? His bed was made up. His beer was brewed. If only he would come!

Laughing and giggling, their dresses wet from being sprayed with water, the girls came out of the garden.

"Domina, we have picked the nicest melons," called Anna and held a bright melon in the air. Critically, Katie looked in the basket.

"Look here, this one is not at all ripe yet! Can you not be careful?" In a bad mood, Katie turned. Did she have to do everything herself? If only she could be in Zuelsdorf. There the heat did not build up between the walls. There one did not have young men standing around on every corner, making faces, whistling at the whores. Even the Doktor would dearly love to leave Wittenberg. Could he not just as well live and work in Zuelsdorf? They would load his books onto the wagon and sell the garden produce in Wittenberg – but the others would not permit it. Not the Elector and not the professors. What would Wittenberg be without him? She stood up to go into the house. What did it help to dream about Zuelsdorf? She would have to remain locked up within these walls.

A noise on the street brought her back to reality.

"Mother, the coach!" Paul tore around the corner with a couple of friends. "Mother, father's coach!" In a cloud of dust, a coach turned into the yard, rattling and creaking. The horses stopped without even a command from the coach driver. Katie's fatigue disappeared.

"Wolf! Jacob! Quickly! Water for the horses! Help them disembark! Where are you? Paul, stay here, you must greet your father!" Paul was already rattling the door of the coach which opened slowly from inside. Wolf hobbled as quickly as he could to help his master. Moaning aloud, Luther pushed his large body out of the coach. As he finally stood on the ground, he held his head with both hands. Katie threw her arms around his neck.

"Oh, my love," moaned Luther, "my excellent wife! How I have suffered! Oh, how tired I am! The streets have all been built by the devil. Those lawyers who love the devil's work so much should ride on them. There isn't a single bone in my body that isn't sore. Support me, Wolf! If God would only save us from every plague!"

Katie walked silently beside him while Wolf and Paul led Luther into the house, where he let himself fall into his chair by the dining room table.

"A drink, dear Katie. Bring me something to drink. I am thirsty enough to drink a horse's trough empty!"

From all sides, the boarders streamed in. The young men earnest, the girls with moral expressions. Luther pushed them away with his hands,

"Off with you; leave me! What you see here is nothing more than a pile of rotting flesh. Go to your work!" He lifted the jug which Katie had brought to his mouth and emptied it with one swig. "Nothing can compare to your beer, my Katie," he said, licking his lips and stroking her hand. "No, I will not travel any more. I am finished. I have been on the road without break for longer than any saint in the old books. No, here I stay. Here it is cool. Close the door, you people! Why do you stand and stare at me? Have you never seen an old man before?" Katie signalled the boarders to leave. Only Wolf and the children stayed sitting at the table. Luther finished a second jug.

"Should I draw you a bath?" Katie asked.

"You are only concerned that I don't bring the bugs and flies from Zeitz and Leipzig into your bed. Do you call that marital love? Did you not promise to share everything with me? But you are right. In the end I had to build a bathroom because my wife is so clean. So, go and draw me a bath, but then – to bed, I beg you." Although Luther joked merrily, Katie looked anxiously into his bloated face. In spite of the heat of summer, his skin had remained pale. His twinkling eyes lay deep in their sockets. As he tried to stand, his chair fell back with a crash. Looking for help, he grabbed for Katie's hand.

That night he groaned and tossed about.

"Oh, Katie, my body! It is as if the devil has already lit the fires of hell in it; as if he was poking his roasting spit into my innards. Oh, no, no!"

Katie sat up. "I will make you a poultice." She took an oil lamp and groped through the dark house into the basement, where she had her herbs suspended. On the tables lay dried manure in various sized basins and in orderly fashion the glasses as they had been organized in Meister Cranach's pharmacy. With the lamp held high in her left hand, she brought the correct amount of powder and herbs together with her right hand and mixed it with a bit of manure. Just as she brought the water to boil on the hearth which was still hot, Dorothea looked around the corner from her room beside the kitchen.

"Domina, what are you doing?"

"The Doktor needs a poultice. His body is as hard as a stone." Dorothea disappeared again. It was quiet in the house until the water finally began to boil quietly.

As morning dawned, Katie continued to sit beside Luther's bed and she changed the cloths which she laid on him.

"Oh, Katie," Luther whispered, "if only I didn't have these doubts. Satan often comes in a dream laughing at me scornfully. And in his hands he swings triumphantly the skulls of the dead who have died for the pure Gospel. Then I hear screams from the graves everywhere: Where is righteousness? And I stand on the pulpit and want to say: With God! But a skeleton's hand closes my mouth so that I begin to feel myself choking." Katie wiped the sweat from his forehead. "Or, I dream that I am sitting at a table and want to write. I hold the quill pen in my hand but blood flows out."

"You torment yourself because the whole world wants something from you. Just think about how much you have already written! Think about the courage and love for the Gospel which has grown in our land. Think about our many faithful friends."

"Friends, yes. But you also know how severely they are tested. Good Spalatin! How he torments himself about the salvation of his soul. And I cannot help him. We are unable to do anything, Katie. God alone can do it but *HE* has apparently turned His back on us. It is with me just as it was with our Lord Jesus Christ as He hung on the cross and asked: *My God, my God, why have you forsaken me?*"

The sun's rays penetrated through the window and made the dust dance in the room. Outside, the birds stirred and then the cock crowed for the third time.

"No, I will not deny *HIM*," sighed Luther. He laid his head to the side and was quiet. After a while it seemed to Katie as if he had fallen asleep. She slipped out of the room and washed her hands and face with cold water. Then she awakened the girls.

───────────

Although snow lay on the roofs outside and was slowly melting, Katie stood in the kitchen sweating. Beside her towered a basket full of freshly baked loaves of bread.

"That should be enough," grumbled Dorothea, shaking her head. "Surely the journey of the gentlemen will not lead through the desert."

"How do you know?" Katie said, rubbing her eyes. "There are four of them besides the two servants. Even if it only lasts to Eisenach, the three boys[66] have good appetites. Thank God, that even Martin is healthy again and eats. Should my sons starve when they accompany their father? Make sure that the herring is prepared for the Doktor." Dorothea shuffled into the basement. Just then, Wolf came into the kitchen.

"The Doktor asks the Domina to send along a small barrel of wine for the road. And you might consider some elderberry petals so that he can make an infusion if it is necessary."

"What? He wants to take along wine? Is he not the guest of the count? But I will look immediately to the elderberry petals." Shaking her head, Katie turned back again to the loaves of bread. There really did seem to be enough. She left the kitchen and mounted the steps to the living room. In the tiled stove, a small fire was burning. Hans, Martin and Paul sat around the table with flushed faces and were studying a map. Katie wrinkled her brow and pushed the paper to the side. Then she sat down between the boys.

"Listen! Even if the weather is mild, put on your warm jackets in the early morning. Sit in the coach so that you do not get a draft. Also, take care that your father doesn't take his coat off, otherwise he will catch a cold. When you stop at an inn, jump out first and call, 'Doktor Martin Luther is coming!' so that the people know who it is and provide a bit of extra care. Before you lay down on your beds, shake the mattress on account of the vermin." Paul gazed out of the window, bored; Martin looked at his mother with large, anxious eyes, and Hans nodded agreement with every sentence.

"Stop preaching, Katie!" Luther, in his shirt and stockings stood in the doorway and held his outer garment in his hand. "I would rather that you sew the hem of my garment so that it will withstand the trip. I fear that the cloth yearns for its deliverance just as much as I do. Oh, I wish I didn't have to travel again!" Upset, he threw the piece of clothing on the bench and said to his sons, "Why are you sitting around? Should you not perhaps be learning something? I hope you won't embarrass me when you need to speak Latin." Katie grabbed the garment and went to the window seat, where she kept her sewing kit.

"If only you could wait until spring," she scolded. "Either it will be so cold that you become sick and have to stay in bed – and who will care for you? Or it will thaw again and the streets will become a muddy mire so that the coach gets stuck or tips."

"Dear Katie! You should not give the devil a detailed catalogue of torments for him to throw at us."

Luther laughed. Katie looked at him surprised. He laughed so seldom now.

"I am loath to see you go, Martinus," she said, bending over her work.

"Nonsense! You concern yourself about your sons! I know that you would love to keep them on your apron strings."

"No, Martinus, not only about them. I am also concerned about you. You speak so much about dying. But I cannot imagine – how I could live without you."

She let her arms sink and looked through the window panes out at the grey sky. With one hand she quickly wiped her eyes. Luther saw it but was too moved to say anything. He crossed the room a couple of times silently, then stood beside her and stroked her shoulder with his hand.

"Katie, my love, everyone has disappointed me; everyone thinks that I am just a ranting, grumbling old man. Even my Philipp has complained to the Elector about me.[67] You're the only one who has held up: God in heaven will reward you. I certainly can't. You know that I have made my will. You shall lack nothing physically even though I did not engage a lawyer to draw it up. Lawyers are only servants of the devil and distort everything. But I cannot do more. God will judge."

Katie laid the garment down and clung to him for a moment.

"Stay with me for a while longer," she whispered. Then she suddenly turned back to her work. The light, which fell through the window pane, had almost faded away.

The next morning at early dawn, all of the boarders stood ready to say farewell to the Doktor. The baskets and jugs were loaded. Katie pulled at the jackets of her sons.

"Hans, you are the oldest! Watch out! And when you see our relatives, greet them from us."

"If it were not for the Mansfeld people who need me, I would stay at home," complained Luther as he mounted the coach.

"I am sure you will be able to settle the matter," said Melanchthon before they closed the door of the coach.[68] The boys stuck their heads out of the back window. Proud and excited they waved to the girls and the boarders. An icy drizzle had begun to fall. Katie pulled her shawl tighter around her shoulders.

"Go inside," she ordered the girls who were standing beside her and waving after the wagon. But she remained in the empty court yard. The coach turned left to the Elbe gate. As she looked after it, Katie saw the horses fall into a slow and steady trot. The heads of the boys disappeared. All that remained was a grey wall of rain and darkness. An ice-cold wind blew across her face.

———————

My dearest homemaker, Katharina Lutherin, Frau Doktor, Owner of Zuelsdorf, pig trader and whatever else. Grace and peace in Christ.

Katie dearest, I became weak on the road shortly before Eisleben; it was my fault. But if you had been here, you would have said it was the fault of the Jews or their God. What's more it is true, as I drove by the village, that such a cold wind blew in from the back of the wagon on my head that it threatened to turn my brain into ice. I drank that tasty Neuburger beer from Mansfeld which you recommended. I enjoyed the taste and it also made me have three bowel movements in three hours. Your dear sons drove to Mansfeld the day before yesterday. I don't know what they were doing there. If it were cold, they would have kept me company as I froze. But since it is warm, they could be doing something else for better or worse as it pleases them. God be with you, together with the whole house. Greet all of the boarders.

On the eve of the Purification of Mary, Martinus Luther, your old love.

Katie refolded the letter and stared out in front of her. The candle on the table had burned slowly down. At length, she grabbed the quill. From the church tower, the clock sounded midnight.

... You should truly be more careful to avoid the wind which blows through the coach. Did I not tell you that you should take along your fur cap? But regarding the beer, buy a little barrel so that some will be left for you when you return; that way we won't need the other remedies when you get constipated again. I am still concerned about your leg. I fear that no doctor will see you to make sure all the pus is removed. I wish you and the children were back home already. At night I lie awake and think about everyone who wishes you ill, the Jews, the Romanists, the unbelievers, the emperor's supporters, and I don't know what to do with all the worries I have on your account. I also pray with tears to the Father in heaven, that He should protect you from the onslaught of the Evil One.

So I hope that your reconciliation efforts with the counts are successful and that you return again soon to your house and your housewife, who awaits you. Your loving, Katharina Lutherin.

She put the writing utensils away. Early in the morning, the messenger would leave. It was so quiet. She heard only the wind blowing around the house. Her eyes almost closed from fatigue but her heart beat with fear for the new day.

———————

"They are coming!" Talking loudly, the children run down the street toward the gate at which a waiting crowd has gathered. A flock of black crows fly away over the Elbe wetland. A few minutes later the bells of St. Mary's and the Castle Church begin to peel. Nothing more can be heard. A thick fog lies over the land. "They are coming!"

Katharina stands rigidly between her sons.

Who is coming? Who could be coming? She gropes with her hand for something to hold on to. Hans supports her. No, she mustn't collapse here before this whole crowd. She must remain standing. What is to become of the children? She must remain standing, even if he — is dead. Why not at home? Why in Eisleben, far from her? Peacefully, they say.[69] Yes, in peace with God, but without saying 'goodbye' to his Katie. They are coming!

Out of the fog, slowly, eerily, several figures appear on horseback. One bears a banner. They ride in formation.[70] They steadily grow in number as more and more people begin to crowd into the street behind her. From every house people come, pressing forward, standing shoulder to shoulder. No one speaks. Only the bells peal across the town. She tries to see. More and more riders appear. The first two reach the gate and stand still. Between them is an opening. Then a wagon approaches and stops. She feels her knees becoming weak. She clings tightly to her sons and tries to breathe quietly.

A driver clothed in black sits on the seat of the coach. The canvas is folded back. A coffin is on it, tightly closed. She would never see his face again. Katharina lets out a soft cry. Melanchthon turns to her. He offers his arm and leads her to a wagon. It is attended by two servants of the mayor. The Count of Mansfeld dismounts from his horse. The council of the town, in full regalia, walks toward him. Katharina does not hear what they say. Listless, she sits down, Margaret beside her. Behind her on a narrow bench sit the wives of their friends. Then the riders begin to move again. The town council and the professors form a row. Only with great difficulty are they able to push back the people. With the bells tolling, the people begin hesitantly to sing as the wagon with the coffin swings before them through the Elster gate. Luther is going home. Katharina's coach follows with her sons close behind her.

"We will see what God will do." That was his last letter.

The bells continue to peal. The riders push their way through the crowd. Women hold their children up to see. Old people stand and weep. The procession stops in front of the castle church. Four men come forward. They lift the coffin down and carry it through the broad open door into the church. Melanchthon helps Katharina from the coach. They follow the pallbearers into the darkness of the church. Hundreds of candles are lit. The singing outside subsides. In front of them, the coffin is carried down the middle aisle, forming a black shadow. The men stop. Katharina notices that in front of the pulpit a grave has been dug in the floor of the church. Behind her she hears a rustling sound as people stream into the church.

"Mother, you should sit down!" Hans helps her to the first pew under the pulpit. In front of her: the hole ... With renewed strength, the congregation begins to sing:

May God to us be gracious;
May we by Him be blessed.
May His face shine upon us;
and bring us to our rest.

---

To Christina von Bora, Grace and Peace from God, the Father of our dear Lord Jesus Christ!

My dear sister.

I appreciate the earnest sympathy which you have for me and my poor children. Who would not be sorrowful and anxious at the death of such a faithful man as my dear husband was, a man who served not only a town or an entire country but the whole world. His death fills me with such sorrow that I can not share it with any other person and I do not know how I will have the courage to get through this. I can neither eat nor drink. Nor can I sleep. If I had a kingdom or an empire, I would not sorrow at losing it nearly as much as I do now that our Lord God has taken away this dear and faithful man from me, and not just from me but from the whole world. When I think about it, God knows, I can neither speak nor write on account of my sorrow and crying, as you, my dear sister, can tell.

Wittenberg, Friday after Oculi,[71] 1546,

Katharina, the widow of Doktor Martinus Luther."

# Between Wittenberg and Dessau, November 1546

Back then, flight from the convent! And now again, flight![72]
Was it not enough, dear Lord, that I had to flee back then?
Was once not enough – the night, the fear, the shaking and
rocking, the bumping of the wheels? It has been more than
twenty years. But the clatter of the wheels, the wind blowing
between the canvas and the wagon box, the freezing cold, the
snorting of the horses – it is now just as it was back then. And
the fear! But how simple it was when I had only myself to
worry about – wedged between the sisters, with wildly
beating hearts. Back then, everyone was afraid for
themselves. This time, my children are pressed at my side. My
children! If they should fall into the hands of the enemy! If the
Spaniards should find them – with their swords and
knives ... No. No, my God. No!

I must not scream. For the children would then become
anxious. They believe that nothing can happen to them as long
as I am with them. Mother, I am not afraid, if you are
here ... Was it Maruschel or Paul? It makes no difference.
They will be quiet as long as I am quiet. But who am I? What
can I do? The imperial soldiers are all over. Murdering
soldiers. Oh, God in heaven, help us! If he was only still here.
If He could come between them and us with the sword of His
Word! They had barely buried him and war broke out. And
everything was in flames.

My children! My poor children! They are Luther's children,
God. You have to protect them for his sake, if the soldiers stop
us on the way, if they drag us from the wagon, if they tear our
clothes from our bodies. Jesus, Mary and all the saints! – He
told the truth. He proclaimed the Gospel pure and
unadulterated. Do not punish us for it, God!

The wagon has stopped. What is wrong? Under no
circumstances should I let myself be seen, Adam had said. He
is a faithful servant. But what can he do against the soldiers? I
hear them speaking. The road is poor. Do we need to get out
of the wagon? It is snowing – so early this year. How will we

*keep warm? Where will I find a roof and bread for my children? Oh, – they are moving, slowly. The horses can't go much farther. Have I ever mistreated them so? The wheels creak ... the wagon leans to one side ... Oh, no!*

*Thank you, Lord Jesus! It is the road, softened by rain and now the snow. The horses have made it. We are going farther, farther into the night – cold, homeless, unprotected, at the mercy of strangers. Will they open their home to us, as I opened my home to fugitives? Or will they be afraid? Will it be too dangerous for them to shelter Luther's wife, Luther's children. ?*

*Behind us lies the Black Monastery. I have always lived in a monastic building. Oh, if we had only gone to Zuelsdorf – you suggested it yourself, Doktor. We could have sat in the orchard in the summer, and now, in the winter, we could be sitting in front of a fire. Only the children and us, not all of the other people, who were always coming and wanting something – "Doktor this ... Doktor that ... "*

*But the soldiers would also come to Zuelsdorf ... We would also have had to flee from there. There is no safe place anymore on earth. They want to capture us, to kill us, to burn us ... for the sake of the Gospel. Yes! God, help us. Do not turn your face from us. Behold the innocent children. Oh, Mother Mary! – Why am I praying to Mary? Yet, he did not forbid it. Indeed he loved her, my Martinus, my Doktor.*

*If he had only been a bit more concerned about money. We could have been rich. I did not want to go about in velvet and furs as Barbara did. But daily bread and a couple of apples, herring and beans. These are the things that I wished for. For these things I worked from morning to night. And then, there was no money when he died. Nothing. I searched through every chest. The last silver goblets I have in my satchel. I will have to sell them to live in Magdeburg or elsewhere. More I don't have. He gave it all away. And he wouldn't accept any money. But when he was dead, the creditors came out of their holes. As long as he was alive, they wouldn't dare. But after he had died, they stood in front of the door of the monastery every day: 'See here, three gulden are still owing for the cow!' 'Could you pay for the boots, Frau Luther? Seven groschen!' If it had not been for the*

*Elector ... He is a good man! Without him we would have been lost. But his chancellor! He called me a quarrelsome woman! He did not acknowledge the will, merely because my Doktor Luther did not use a lawyer for it.[73] He wanted to take away my children – Oh, how I fought! Paul is sleeping. Maruschel is weeping because we had to leave Toelpel behind. Old Wolf will care for him. He doesn't have anything else to do in the empty house.*

*If Hans would only study a little harder. Everyone is always dissatisfied with him.*

*'Mother, I can't do any better,' he says. Is it his fault? But the chancellor thinks that it is my fault and that they should take all of them away from me. They play too much. As though their father was not strict enough! Should I too have been drilling them all day long? It is hard to raise children to be decent, hardworking people when the devil motivates people everywhere. So they named guardians for the children. Because their mother can't do it. And now? Now we are fleeing and don't know where to go. And the guardians – they also have to flee.*

*Is Adam never going to stop? Are we still not safe? How are we to find the road to Dessau in the middle of the night? It is so cold. Martin has only just become well again. He will catch another cold. Paul is also coughing. If they come down with a fever – I have nothing that I can give them. If only I had brought along the satchel with the elderberry petals! What will happen to my pharmacy? Take they my life, goods, child and wife. [74] Yes, my dear Doktor. We will gladly sing it but when it comes to that, it is hard and the children ... No, Lord Jesus, do not ask that of me, not my children!*

*Oh, how little faith, I have. Forgive your Katie, my dear Doktor up there in heaven. Forgive her. I know I must have more confidence – after all, I have already experienced what it means to flee. And did not God's angel guide us? Was it not also bitterly cold and dark that night? And the bumping of the wagon – did it not also jar each of us? We did not know what was going to happen and did not everything go well for us, so well?*

# Wittenberg, 1547-1552

The horses stopped. Katie carefully moved her cramped legs and got down from the coach box.[75] She looked around her. The walls of the Black Monastery were standing. That was enough to start with. She turned to the two horses and patted the neck of the favourite one. The mare looked at her as though she understood. The long journey was at an end. Her eyes closed. Her nostrils trembled. How thin she is, thought Katharina.

"Get off," called Katharina to the children. "Above all, give attention to the horses! Where is Wolf?" She looked around. The old man should have been limping across the courtyard. Instead, a young maid from Melanchthon's house came down the street out of breath.

"Frau Doktor, I am to bid you welcome. And, in case you did not get the letter from the Meister, no one is living in the house anymore. Wolf has died."

The children raced into the garden. Katharina went over to the pear tree. The leaves above her rustled. It was so quiet that she could hear it speak – of the olden days and the joyful life.

"Toelpel, Toelpel! Why is Toelpel not here?" Maruschel came back crying and threw herself into her mother's arms. Paul stood with lips pressed tightly together at the door of the house. Inside it was dark and empty. It smelled of death.

"Lead me to my bench," said Katharina, leaning on Margaret's thin shoulder. Her dress rustled as she let herself down. 1540 was clearly readable over the sandstone gate. But the place on the other side was empty.

"Are you all right?" Maruschel asked anxiously.

"Oh, child ..." She wiped her tears with her soiled sleeve. Margaret looked around not knowing what to do.

"Are they all dead, Mother?" The babble of voices came nearer from down the street. They could hear Melanchthon speaking in his soft distinctive voice. Several women followed, carrying baskets and accompanied by children.

"No, no," said Katharina and stood up. She smoothed out her dress and threw back her head. "No, no, Maruschel, we are still living."

---

"God has noticeably kept His hand over Wittenberg. Otherwise, dear Frau Doktor, you would not have found your house and the surrounding gardens unharmed," said Philippe, as everyone sat around the table in the house of Melanchthon that evening. "I saw everything burned to the ground outside the walls." They ate their soup silently. "No Spanish soldier set foot in the town. Only Duke Alba. And they did not desecrate the grave of our dear Martinus. It was altogether different in Eger, where the followers of the emperor cut off the hands and feet of the children of the Evangelicals ..."

"Stop it, Philippus," growled Melanchthon's wife.

"I will see tomorrow what is still growing in the gardens. The children will help me." Katharina laid her spoon down and wiped her mouth. "Then, the students will certainly come again. I have as many rooms as before." Melanchthon smiled.

"You are right not to despair, Frau Doktor. Your Lord would have been pleased at this ..."

Later, Martin stood with an empty bucket in the kitchen and looked at his mother.

"There are no more fish in the pond, not even one. And the trees ..." He swallowed hard. Katharina cast a look at his pale face. He had the dark eyes of his father but there was no fire glowing in them. Good, she thought. One Luther was already too many for this world. She turned again to her dough.

"We will plant new trees," she said slowly and her fingers dug down deep into the piece of dough made of flour and eggs. "Now go to the market and see what there is to buy. If you meet up with anyone you know, ask whether Dorothea is still in Wittenberg and give them the message that she can cook for us again – God will repay her; I cannot, but you don't have to say that. And if there is fruit to be bought, bring some and tell them they should charge it. Luther's wife will pay for it – later. Or the King of Denmark will pay for it. At least, that's what he promised." [76]

She pressed the piece of dough together vigorously and then put it on the table to roll. "But of course, you don't tell them that. Act as if we have the money. Surely, they can't let us starve." Martin looked at the floor. Then he went slowly to the door. "Take Maruschel along!," called Katharina after him. "She can speak better than you. And don't forget who you are! You are Luther's son!" She sobbed as the door closed.

---

To my dear mother, widow of the famous Doktor Martinus Luther, Frau Katharina Lutherin at Wittenberg. Grace and peace from God and our Lord Jesus Christ, Amen.

Dear mother,

We arrived in Leipzig safe and sound on the 30th. The town was hot and sticky. Since then, however, a strong rain has fallen and the streets have become a muddy mire. In spite of this, you need not worry about me; my shoes are solid and waterproof. The day after our arrival we went immediately to the courts. I presented myself as a lawyer with my attestation from the University of Koenigsberg[77] and was accepted with great courtesy. Doktor Stramburger, who guided your court case so successfully against Herr Von Kieritzsch filled me in on the process of the proceedings. I also met up with your dear brother, who enumerated the extent of the damages which the troops of Marshall Loeser inflicted upon your property. Then on 2nd July, faithful Adam von Zuelsdorf arrived and related with tears in his eyes how the soldiers caused havoc, worse than the plague, and how they did not leave a single pig alive but butchered and carried off everything. They even broke into the cellar and cleaned out everything there.[78]

Then with Adam we went before the courts again. However, we had to wait a long time and are postponed for the present time. Adam wants to return home again since old Josepha, who is half blind, is alone in the house. Only the large house is still standing. Adam says that everything else is torn down or burned to the ground, partly through the war and partly from the soldiers of the liberator, who did not show his thanks for the honour which our blessed father showed his father, the old field marshal, when he asked him to be the godfather for my dear brother. I am told that he is high and mighty and not at all sorry for the damages which he inflicted on your property. I have high hopes that our faithful friends will support us. If not, I do not know how we can save anything of the small estate. Adam would again buy a couple of cows if you could give him the money. Magister Kram asked me to give you 400 gulden. He said that he would gladly loan the widow of Doktor Martinus Luther some money if she needs it. Tell me what answer I should give him.

I have been asked to send greetings from all the friends whom you visited on your trip two years ago. I have also heard that your dear fellow sister Elsa von Canitz has died after a long illness. She lived right to the end in her little house near the girls' school at Grimma, where she had faithfully taught the Gospel as our blessed father wished. The friends tell me that the work which she established with sister Magdalena flourishes under the blessing of the Lord. Therefore you should not grieve but praise the Lord for her God-pleasing life.

Soon, dear mother, I hope to be able to give you a better report on the proceedings in the courts. But it will be difficult to wrest compensation from the marshal. This is not only because your claim is being challenged concerning your rights to Zuelsdorf, despite the verdict which you won two years ago, but also because people depict you here as a litigious woman. All of our friends go out of their way to contradict this but, unfortunately, we have too many enemies.

So stay well, dear mother, and greet my dear Elisabeth, who certainly still needs your help and advice as she prepares for our wedding. I hope soon to return to you. I

don't have much yearning to travel since I
know how much you worry. So do not be
concerned any further but be of good cheer.
God's grace be with you and with those in
your house.

Leipzig, 10 July, 1552.
Your dear son,
Johannes (Hans) Luther.

It had become dark. Katharina laid the letter on the
table under the flickering candle. Naturally she would
care for Elisabeth. The delicate young woman had
little ability for work. Even her own father, old
Cruciger, agreed that she would probably not be able
to manage a household. The night was sultry.
Katharina wiped the perspiration from her forehead
and slowly loosened her kerchief. Her long hair, which
had become grey, fell onto the table top. Through the
open window came a draft of air which blew it about
slightly. Who else still saw this hair which Doktor
Martinus loved to stroke? She sighed a little.

Oh, if she had only been in Leipzig herself, she
would have made it hot for those men. She knew how
to defend her rights, even without studying law.
Litigious woman – they can talk. It didn't make any
difference to her. But Hans! He would move across the
paper with his fine thin hands. With soft, somewhat
complaining voice, he would point to this or that. How
different children often are from their parents!

A bird of the night called. Upstairs in the rooms of
the students it was quiet. Perhaps one or the other was
still studying but most of them were not very diligent.
They would rather chase after Maruschel. Yes,
whoever gets her will have a capable wife. But she was
still too young. She should wait. How her father would
have ranted if a rumour had come to his ears. He
would have ... like that time with his niece Lena – that
was terrible – So many memories. Cruciger sat here at
the table. Bent over the Bible. Luther beside him.

Jonas and she, Katie, by the window, after she had come out of the kitchen, where the maids clattered with the dishes and Dorothea maintained an iron regime, where the children always screamed and the wind blew through the chimney ... like now.

Two young men in white clothes suddenly stood in the middle of the room. "What are you looking for?" Katharina asked the two.

They smiled and looked at each other. "Do you not know who we are, Frau Doktor?"

"Yes, certainly! I know who you are. You came to me back then. "

"We came when you watched over the bed of your little Lena."

"You took her from me!"

"We brought her to her Father in heaven."

"And who do you want to take now? No! No! So many have died. Leave me my children! Do not take everything from me. God in heaven, help!"

The men were silent and turned, still smiling, toward the door. Katharina got up.

"Oh, it is you, Magister!" Melanchthon was standing in the shadows beside the table.

"Pardon me, Frau Doktor, I know it is late in the night. I knocked but you must have fallen asleep."

"Here, read!" said Katharina. She pushed the letter to him and groped for the candle.

Melanchthon put up his hand. "No, I can't stay. You have to pack up – the plague!"

Katharina shook her head vehemently.

"Yes. Yes," Melanchthon continued softly and imploringly. "Your house is threatened too, Katharina, tomorrow our faculty will also pack up for Torgau.[79] Your son Martin will go with us."[80]

"And the medical doctors?"

"They have decided to remain."

"So Paul[81] cannot go along?"

"No."

"Then I will stay also."

A storm rolled over the Elbe. The moon, which still provided a little light, vanished behind dark threatening clouds. Melanchthon lifted his hands helplessly.

"Pack your things!"

The door slammed behind him. Katharina heard him go through the house. She remembered the two men. She felt chilly. The window banged closed.

"Frau Doktor!" The calls came from upstairs. Someone came down the stairs. "Frau Doktor! Young Jacob has a fever! Could you come? He has red spots in his face."

"Mother!" Martin also stood in the room. He held a weak light in his hands. His voice quivered: "Mother, is this the plague?"

Katharina suddenly realized how tired she was.

---

An autumn fog lay over the Elbe river and rose in thick clouds into the yard of the Black Monastery. Two coaches stood there, one for the few boarders who had stayed, one for the Luther family. Katharina groaned as she mounted the steps one last time to the first floor. She dug around in the trunk under her seat by the window and pulled out the linen bag in which she kept her sewing and Luther's glasses. She hid her treasure in the folds of her large dress. But she remained standing by the door as she was about to leave. The early light of dawn came through the window panes. In the corner the tile stove reflected the light. The floorboards were scrubbed and polished, the wooden trim on the walls artistically decorated. Katharina smiled sadly. How cosy she had made the half-ruined monastery building! If only she did not have to leave it again! Why could she not remain sitting at the table? Yes, where Doktor Luther had sat in front of her, with the Bible open? Why must she leave again, travel the roads, as a refugee with her children ... ? If she was alone in the world, she would stay, yes, she would stay. But for the plague to come into her house three times, that was too much.

The door closed with a soft groan. Katharina came down as quickly as she could. Her grey dress dragged audibly over the stairs. Otherwise, everything was quiet. Outside, she bolted the door to the house and cast a glance at the empty stone seats on the right and left of the gate. The boarders had already got into the coach. A cool wind blew through the manes of the horses. Eager to take charge, Paul held the reins in his hands. "Paul, you can't handle that!" Old Urban got on the seat of the coach box and Paul moved obediently to the side. With some difficulty, Katharina climbed up too and sat beside them. Maruschel sat behind them and waved to the students in the second wagon. The grey sky in the east was broken by a ray of the sun.

As the coach started to move with a jerk, Katharina pulled her shawl tighter around herself. Cold sweat stood on her forehead, in spite of the autumn cool. She looked straight ahead. The yard which they left behind was empty. The first leaves were falling from the pear tree.

# Torgau, December 1552

"Maruschel, is it not yet morning?"

"No, mother, it is still the middle of the night."

"Oh, the pain, the pain.[82] Oh, that my Lord Christ would rescue me! If I could only move. Child!"

"Yes, mother?" "What did the doctor say? Did he say that there was no hope?"

"He said, we must place ourselves under God's will."

"If only I could go to the toilet myself. But I cannot do it. All my bones must be broken from the fall."

"I will help you, mother. Should I bring you the bed pan?"

"No, child, no. You must sleep. Why am I bothering you in the middle of the night? If I could only close my eyes. But every part of my body is burning like hellfire. And at the same time, I am so cold."

"I will get you a new brick from the stove and lay it on your feet."

"Thank you. Thank you! Warmth! Yes, I was often so cold in the monastery – and then it was so pleasant by the oven in our room. Wasn't it so, Maruschel?"

"Yes, mother. We had it nice in the winter, nice and warm. And then when father took out his lute ... "

"I got a lot of joy from the way you sang. Oh, if I was only with our dear father. I wonder if he also plays his lute in heaven and if the angels sing with him? My Doktor! I would not have guessed that I could have loved him so much. He was so good. If I only did not have this pain, I would praise God without ceasing. But it is hard for me. Why must I have such pain? I would just love to move around and work but I lie here – Maruschel, how long has it been already? How long?"

"It was in September when you tumbled into the trench. Now it is a few days before Christmas."

"So long, already. So long, already! I wanted to flee from the plague—and now the plague has long since gone and I cannot go back. Your father once said that it is not sinful to flee from the plague but the Lord God above is still punishing me. He has taken everything from me: my property, my Zuelsdorf, my gardens, everything destroyed, no cattle anymore, no fields, and now I lie here – but I know: it must be this way so that we do not hang our hearts on things.

"And yet, when I die, do not forget who you are! You can be proud — and if a son of a prince were to ask for your hand, he would only just be good enough for you.[83] How your father loved you! When his Lenchen died, you were his comfort and his joy. With his sons he was often harsh and stern. Oh, too stern, I often thought. But you he held in his arms and kissed. Do not forget it. Princes trembled in front of this man. He withstood the pope in Rome. Even the emperor – but what help is that for my pain? How small we become in the face of our Lord God, when He allows us to suffer like this. I wish I could call to all the saints. But they cannot help me. Nothing can help.

"If only they preserve the pure doctrine! Give heed to that, Maruschel, when you marry a clever man, that he helps to proclaim the Gospel properly. As our dear father taught us. There is so much hatred and strife. And our good Philippus. He often wavers like a reed in the wind. Then someone comes and says, Good works – yes. And another says, Good works – no. I do not understand the argument. If they were lying here like I am, they would not argue about such things. They would instead stretch out their hand into the dark night to see if there might not be somebody there who would take it.

"Child, child, how come I tumbled so fearfully? Why could Urban not stop the horses?"

"He is too old, mother. Perhaps dear Paul should have taken the reins."

"No, I should have taken them. But I jumped down and thought I was still young and strong and could stop the horses. I forgot how old I was, Maruschel. Do not forget when you are older and have given birth to children that you have to rest up a bit. I couldn't. There was always so much to do but I don't regret it. I'm not sorry. No, it was good. And God made certain that I did not become arrogant. 'With our might is nothing done … ' I wish I could read once more from my hymnal."

"Should I light a candle?"

"No, no, tomorrow morning I will get my book and father's glasses, then I will read. No, I want to sleep but I cannot. If I could only move my body to lie in a different position. My back is so painful. No, you cannot help me, dear child. Go to sleep. Go and lie down! I want to be quiet now.

"Oh, my Lord Christ, when you would pass by, I would not only want to touch Your garment. I would want to stick like a burr to your garment. Help me. Help me! When will it be morning?"

———————

Throughout Torgau the bells peel.

"It is Luther's wife," whisper people to each other. "The one who was a nun … that time on Easter morning?"

"Yes, she is the one. She was bedridden for a long time," says one to the other.

"She must have been very ill."

"No, she tumbled off a coach. The horses bolted as they came from Wittenberg."

"She died this morning, according to the baker. It happened as the first light shone into her window."

"See, her sons are coming."

"One is missing."

"If the good Elector still lived, there would be a large funeral."

People disperse into the streets. The sky becomes overcast. Slushy snow lies on the cobble stones. The pallbearers have to take care not to slip. The casket sways on their shoulders. It is not far. In the town church the organ plays. A small group passes through the open door into the dim light. Shivering, the mourners stand around the grave dug into the altar area. Hesitant singing fills the vaulted building. The bells stop ringing, one after the other.[84]

# Translator's Notes

1    Luther called Katie "the morning star of Wittenberg" since she started her days promptly at 4 a.m.

2    The Augustinian cloister in Wittenberg, valued at 6,000 gulden ($450,000) in Luther's time, which Elector Frederick of Saxony gave to Martin and Katharina Luther (before his death and which Elector John had renovated) when they got married in 1525. This is where the Luthers and their extended family, along with many students and guests, lived. In 1564, the Luther children sold it to the university for $277,500.

3    We have kept the German formal expression "Herr Doktor" which denotes respect. English tends to be less formal than German anyway and so that in the absence of a natural translation. we have transliterated certain expressions to give a German flavor to the whole.

4    Wolfgang Seberger, Luther's household servant.

5    For a basic historical account of Katharina's life, one must rely chiefly on her husband's letters and his Table Talks, some independent historical accounts, letters by contemporaries, and the text of some of her surviving letters. Katharina was the daughter of Hans von Bora and Katharina von Haubitz, both of noble descent. The von Bora family had once been the Margraves of Meissen. While the members of Katharina's immediate family owned land, they were not wealthy. Most of the novitiates and nuns in the Nimbschen cloister were of similar noble extraction.

6    Katharina's mother died in 1504 when Katharina was five years of age and Katharina was sent to be educated at the Benedictine convent school at Brehna. Katharina's father remarried in 1505 and four years later, as was common for "adolescent virgins" of noble descent, Katharina entered the Cistercian cloister of Marienthron at Nimbschen in Ducal Saxony.

7    A gulden was a coin valued at $75.00, a substantial amount in those days.

8    The nuns in Brehna were Benedictines which kept the rules of poverty, chastity and obedience but were not as strict as some other orders. For example, the nuns were not strictly enclosed.

9    The Cisterians were a reform order founded to counteract the laxity of the Benedictines. They were also called "white monks" because of the colour of their habit.

10    St. Bernard of Clairvaux (1091-1153) spent himself on ascetic practices and was known for his glorification of Mary.

11    This was likely Margaret von Haubitz, identified in a census of the inhabitants of Marienthron from 1509-1520. Actually, Katharina was five when her mother died. A rood screen separated the choir where the nuns would worship from the rest of the congregation.

12    In the sixteenth century, when the marriageable age for girls was much lower than it is today, it would not have been unusual for girls to begin their novitiate at age fourteen or fifteen.

13    St. Francis of Assissi, the founder of the Franciscan order of friars.

14    St. Clare of Assissi, converted under the influence of St. Francis in 1212.

15    By the sixteenth century, most churches and monasteries had a collection of relics, i.e. items which purported to be connected with Christ or one of the saints. People who viewed these relics, prayed before them and paid a certain amount of money, were held to have done a good work for which they were granted indulgences. Some of the money from the sale of indulgences went to support the church or monastery where the relics were located. It was the abuses which arose from the sale of indulgences which sparked the Reformation.

16    A likely reference to Martin Luther who took issue with indulgences with his posting of his 95 Theses on the castle door in Wittenberg on October 31, 1517. Johannes Cochlaeus, Luther's fierce foe and first biographer, characterized Luther in 1529 as having seven heads. He called him an agent of the devil, a perversion, and a monster.

17    The passage which Katharina is reading is from *The Freedom of a Christian* written by Luther in November 1520. The text follows the translation in the American Edition of Luther's Works, 31: 345.

18    Martin Luther preached in the town of Grimma as early as 1519.

19    Wolfgang von Zeschau, prior of the Augustinian Hermits in Grimma, who left that monastery with a number of monks in 1522.

20    The Freedom of the Christian, 344.

21    Sister of John Staupitz, Luther's superior, Vicar of the German congregation of the Augustinian Order, one of the founders of the University of Wittenberg.

22    It was a dangerous undertaking to liberate nuns. According to both Canon and Civil Law the offender might expect the

death penalty. However, the authorities from Ducal Saxony, which were hostile to Luther, had no means of stopping the vehicle once it was under way since it quickly crossed the border into Electoral Saxony.

23   Merchant and alderman Leonhard Koppe of Torgau, on the evening of April 4, 1523 spirited nine nuns out of the territory of Duke George, a strong opponent of Luther, to safety in the territory of Luther's protector, Elector Frederick the Wise. Among them were Katharina von Bora, Ave and Margaret von Schoenfeld, and Margaret and Veronika von Zeschau. In a published open letter to Leonhard Koppe, entitled *Why Nuns May Leave Cloisters with God's Blessings* (1523), Luther accepted responsibility for the rescue and for the destitute women.

24   Elector Frederick the Wise had his main residence in Torgau.

25   Although the Elector lived in Torgau, which had a population of 2,700, Wittenberg, with a population of only 2,300, was the principal city in Electoral Saxony. Frederick the Wise undertook to beautify Wittenberg, completely rebuilding the Castle and the Castle Church into a structure of Gothic beauty, employing the best artists of the day to decorate the interior. He rebuilt the Rathaus in a new Renaissance style. Homes were also built for the more important professors teaching in the new University of Wittenberg, founded in 1502.

26   Philipp Melanchthon (Schwarzerd), born February 16, 1497 in Baden, arrived to teach at the University of Wittenberg on August 25, 1518 and became a close co-worker of Luther in the Reformation movement. He died April 19, 1560. The German title "Magister," for which there is no adequate corresponding title in English, is applied to him. It's something close to Professor.

27   Between 1323 and 1409, Wittenberg had constructed a complete system of fortifications considered excellent for that day. These included a wide moat, a stone wall, and raised embankments. It was considered a desirable place of residence and soon developed into the principal city of Electoral Saxony.

28   Melanchthon had married Katharina Krapp, the daughter of the mayor of Wittenberg on November 25, 1520.

29   Jerome Baumgaertner, son of a distinguished patrician family in Nurenberg, who studied in Wittenberg from 1518 to 1521. In 1523 he revisited Wittenberg and met Katharina at that time.

30   Joachim Camerarius was a professor in Wittenberg, who was a good friend of Melanchthon and a close associate of Luther at Wittenberg.

31  St. Catharine of Sienna (1347-1380) led an ascetic life and was known for her devotion and piety.

32  The Reformation painter, Lucas Cranach the Elder, owned considerable property in Wittenberg, including the drugstore in which spices, wax, paint, and paper were sold in addition to drugs. The town records show that by 1528 he owned four houses and a number of gardens and fields. He was so respected by his fellow citizens that between 1535 and 1544 he was mayor of the town.

33  Frederick the Wise died in May 1525 and was succeeded as elector by his brother John the Constant.

34  King Christian II of Denmark and Norway (1481-1559), nephew of Elector Frederick the Wise, attempted to reform the University of Copenhagen in a humanist direction and effectively began the movement toward Lutheranism in Scandinavia. In 1523, he went into voluntary exile in Germany where he became a committed Lutheran. Luther supported the king politically and condemned his Danish subjects for betraying their God-appointed lay authority.

35  In his attempt to subdue the Swedes who had set up their own monarchy, Christian had eighty Swedish nobles killed November 8-10, 1520 in what became known as the 'Stockholm Blood Bath'.

36  The Peasants' Revolt began in the Black Forest on May 30, 1524 and in April, 1525, Luther had expressed sympathy for some of their demands in his tract Admonition to Peace in Response to the Twelve Articles. However, already in this tract, he accused them of confusing the Gospel and human rights.

37  Kasper Glatz, former rector of the University of Wittenberg, was not popular with his colleagues who regarded him as somewhat miserly.

38  In addition to the frequent open-air markets held several times a week, Wittenberg witnessed grander events twice a year which reached the proportions of a medieval fair. On those occasions, guilds presented plays on specially built platforms.

39  Nicholaus von Amsdorf (1483-1565) lectured with Luther at the University of Wittenberg. In 1524, he was called to Magdeburg.

40  Luther showed great concern when the peasants resorted to violence. In the heat of conflict, he wrote *Against the Murdering Hordes of Peasants* in which he insisted that it was the prince's duty, as God's sword on earth, to suppress all revolt. The princes needed no encouragement to move with great severity against the peasants.

41  1 Kings 17:1-6.

42 Luther continued to preach in the revolutionary centres, despite the insults of the masses.

43 Justus Jonas (1493-1555) was the Probst (provost) of the Castle Church and a close colleague of Luther at the University of Wittenberg.

44 June 13, 1525. According to contemporary custom, a German wedding consisted of two parts, a small private wedding which involved only the official participants, the pastor, and witnesses, and later the blessing of the couple in the Town Church, followed by an elaborate party for relatives and guests.

45 The public service to mark the marriage took place in the Town Church on June 27, 1525. The ceremony was followed by a special wedding banquet at the Black Monastery in the afternoon and an Ehrentanz, a kind of square dance, in the basement of the Rathaus (town hall) in the evening. The Elector John sent a gift of $7,500 to help the couple get started and the Town Council sent $1,500 to help defray the cost of the wedding banquet.

46 Proverbs 31:10-31.

47 To retain the rhyme form, slight liberties in translation from the German are taken.

48 Luther introduced German into the liturgy gradually, retaining some old forms with the new.

49 June 7, 1526.

50 Psalm 91:7.

51 December 10, 1527.

52 Elizabeth died on August 3, 1528 at the age of seven months.

53 While Elector John and other Lutheran princes and theologians went to Augsburg to take a stand for Lutheranism at the Diet, it was not safe for Luther to leave the territory of the Elector; Coburg was as far south as he could go. From there he kept daily contact with his colleagues at the Diet.

54 Magdalena was born on May 4, 1529.

55 Born January 29, 1533.

56 Born November 9, 1531

57 Margarethe was born on December 17, 1534.

58 In a controversy which erupted after Luther's death, Agricola objected to the statement: 'One must do good works', because he took the word must (debitum) to mean 'coerced by fear of punishment.'

59 Aunt Lena died in 1537.

60 A German form of endearment for the name Margaret.

61 A German term of endearment for the name Magdalena.

62    Unable to maintain normal conjugal relations with his wife, whom he had married when he was nineteen years old, Philipp had lived a grossly immoral life for which he felt little remorse until he came under the influence of Luther. In The Babylonian Captivity (1520), Luther had said that bigamy was not so serious an offense as divorce and early in 1540 when Philip decided he wanted to marry Margaret von der Saul, Luther, Melanchthon and Martin Bucer reluctantly agreed that a pastor might make an exception to the law and permit bigamy in order to correct a greater evil.

63    Luther assumed that things would be kept secret on the principle that confidences given and advice received in the confessional were to be held inviolable by both parties. Philipp, however, did not adhere to this principle and Luther's advice became another point where his adversaries attacked him.

64    Also referred to as a 'Turkish marriage,' this expression described a secret second marriage when a man was already officially married to another woman.

65    In 1544, Luther valued the Zuelsdorf property at $45,750.

66    In later life, Luther suffered physically from his earlier rigorous monastic disciplines and fastings. The many demands upon his time as professor and pastor, and the nervous tension of being constantly in the public eye, combined to take a further toll from his physical stamina. In 1537, he also suffered a severe gall bladder attack.

67    George Spalatin, Court chaplain, historian, secretary, and confidential advisor to Elector Frederick the Wise and his successors, was a strong supporter of the Reformation.

68    E. G. Schwiebert, Luther and His Times, p. 749 indicates that only Martin and Paul accompanied their father to Eisleben.

69    In his funeral oration at Luther's death, Melanchton praised him but also added a note of criticism, suggesting that Luther had had rough edges and negative qualities.

70    Late in 1545 the princes of Mansfeld engaged in a bitter family quarrel, which Luther was asked to arbitrate. Although Luther was not eager to undertake the journey of about eighty miles, in the midst of winter, his strong sense of duty and consideration of his home country finally persuaded him to attempt the task.

71    After three trying weeks, the dispute was finally settled amicably on February 17. That evening and throughout the night, Luther suffered three heart attacks. Early in the morning on February 18 as he was growing steadily weaker, his friend Justus Jonas asked him, "Reverend Father, are you willing to die in the name of the Christ and the doctrine which you have preached?" to which Luther replied "Yes"

so distinctly that the whole group attending him heard it. He then fell asleep and did not awaken.

72    A funeral service was held in Eisleben on February 19 and a memorial service on February 20. A funeral procession then began under escort of the officials of the Duke of Mansfeld. At Bitterfeld on the border of Electoral Saxony, they were relieved by the Elector John Frederick's officials who provided an escort to Wittenberg. After a long and mournful journey, with church bells ringing and crowds of people gathering along the route, Luther's body reached Wittenberg on February 22. Leading the procession to Wittenberg were two mounted knights, accompanied by sixty horsemen preceding the hearse.

73    The third Sunday in Lent.

74    On June 16, 1546, the Schmalcald War broke out between the Protestants and the forces of Emperor Charles V. For several months, the opposing armies faced each other across the Danube without a major engagement. Then Moritz, the Lutheran ruler of Ducal Saxony, joined forces with the Emperor, bribed by the promise of the Electoral title. In the middle of winter, Katie and her children fled to Magdeburg.

75    Luther made two wills. The first was in 1537 when he became seriously ill and thought he might die. It was drawn up mainly to protect Katharina against lawyers of the Saxon court who might take away her sons as minors. The will called upon Melanchthon, Jonas and Cruciger to protect her in that case. Luther felt that she was a capable mother and manager of her family. Luther's second will was drafted in 1542, written in his own handwriting, and legally recorded in 1544. In it he listed all his property, all of which he bequeathed to Katharina, and indicated that he trusted her more than lawyers to be the custodian of their children.

76    The customary law in the Saxonspiegel relegated wives to maids without legal status. Thus, Chancellor Brueck insisted that the boys should be taken away from her in order to receive proper training. With the help of Melanchthon and Cruciger, she finally persuaded the chancellor that Hans had no talent for the law and that the two professors were capable of instructing the two younger boys.

77    Translation follows the words of the English rendition of the hymn *A Mighty Fortress.*

78    In the spring of 1547, the forces of the Emperor and Duke Moritz defeated the troops of Elector John Fredrick who was taken captive. Katie and her family, accompanied by the wife of Bugenhagen, fled to Magdeburg a second time. On May 19, 1547, Wittenberg capitulated and Moritz became the new Elector of Saxony. Since he promised security and peace to the town and University, the faculty gradually

returned. In the latter part of June, Katie also felt obligated to return.

79     The King of Denmark had promised to send 50 thaler per year (a substantial amount) for Katie's maintenance.

80     The Duke of Prussia stood by Katie and provided Hans with an education at the University of Koenigsberg.

81     Katie's farm lay right along the highway used by both armies in the war. Her livestock disappeared and her barns and sheds were pillaged and burned.

82     In the summer of 1552, when the plague again broke out in Wittenberg, the University moved to Torgau. By fall, Katie decided to leave also.

83     Martin, 21, studied theology but never occupied a pulpit.

84     Paul, 19, studied medicine and later became a prominent family physician.

85     On the way to Torgau, the horses became frightened and bolted. Katie jumped from the carriage and was badly hurt when she fell. For months she lay between life and death before she finally died on December 20, 1552, aged 53 years, 11 months.

86     Margaret married Georg von Kunheim from a rich Prussian noble family on August 5, 1555. She died however at the age of 36 in 1570.

87     Owing to the unsettled conditions, Katie was buried in Torgau instead of near her husband.

# Dates and Facts
## (research by the author)

| | |
|---|---|
| 29th January 1499 | Katharina von Bora [K.] was born to Hans von Bora in Lippendorf. Her mother died soon afterwards. |
| 1505 | K. Is taken to a convent school run by Benedictine nuns in Brehn. |
| 1509 | K. enters Marienthron, a convent run by Cistercian nuns, in Nimbschen, where an aunt on her mother's side is Mother Superior, and where a sister of her father, Magdalena von Bora, lives. |
| 1515 | After one year as a novice K. Takes her vows and becomes a nun. |
| 4th/5th April 1523 | During the Easter night K is taken, together with eight other nuns, from Nimbschen to Torgau, by Leonhard Koppe. A few days later, the nuns are in Wittenberg. |
| 1523 - 1525 | K gets to know king Christian II of Denmark in the house of the Painter Lucas Cranach Hieronymus Baumgaertner von Nuerenberg promises to marry her, but fails to remain get in touch with her. Luther writes a letter to him to enquire about this matter. |
| 13th June 1525 | K and Luther marry. |
| 27th June 1525 | The marriage is officially celebrated with a church service. Foreign guests attend. |
| 1525 or 26 | Magdalena von Bora (Aunt Lena) comes to live in the house. |
| 7th June 1526 | Johannes Luther is born. |
| 1527 | An epidemic of the plague breaks out in Wittenberg. Luther and his wife stay. |

| | |
|---|---|
| 10th December 1527 | Elisabeth Luther is born. |
| 3rd August 1528 | Elisabeth dies. |
| 4th May 1529 | Magdalene Luther (Lenchen) is born. |
| April to October 1530 | Luther stays at the fortress in Coburg. At the same time Parliament is in session in Augsburg. He regularly writes to his family. |
| 9th November 1531 | Martin Luther (jnr) is born. |
| 1532 | Luther buys for Katharina the garden by the pigs' market; and finishes the first Bible translation, which is being revised by other theologians in Wittenberg in the coming years. |
| 28th January 1533 | Paul Luther is born. |
| 17th December 1534 | Margarete Luther (Maruschel) is born. It is exceptionally cold. |
| 1535 | The Luther lounge in the "black monastary" is being enlarged and a bit later a bathroom is enlarged too. There are eight orphans from Luther's family living in the house, together with Luther's natural children. Two girls are called Else and Lene. A bit later children from K.s family join as well. They play with a dog called Toelpel. |
| 1537 | Painter Lucas Cranach's son, Hans, dies in Bologna. Aunt Lena dies. The psychologically ill electoral princess of Brandenburg is being cared for at the Black Monastery. |
| 1539 | There is another outbreak of the Plague in Wittenberg. Luther and K. take in four children of the deceased Muenster couple. |

| | |
|---|---|
| January 1540 | Luther buys the Zuelsdorf property from brother Hans von Bora for K. after her recovery. There is unrest amongst the Protestants due to Luther's and Melanchthon's advice to Philipp of Hesse, regarding his "double marriage". |
| November 1540 | K. presents Luther with a birthday gift which is the sandstone portal by the Black Monastery with the two alcoves to sit on and a relief. |
| Summer 1541 | K stays in Zuelsdorf for such a long time, that Luther asks her in a letter, delivered to her by the servant Urban, to return. Rosina, supposedly a nun to whom certain housekeeping tasks were entrusted, turns out to be a swindler. |
| January 1542 | Luther makes his will in which K., contrary to common law, is the beneficiary. |
| September 1542 | Lenchen is very sick. In Torgau Hans is asked to come to the sick bed. K tells Melanchthon of a dream: Two men came to take Lenchen to the wedding. |
| 20th September 1542 | Lenchen dies. |
| August 1544 | Luther travels to Zeitz and returns exhausted. |
| 1545 | Melanchthon complains about Luther's excessive anger. Luther proposes that K. leave Wittenberg. |
| 23rd January 1546 | Luther starts for Eisleben together with his three sons in order to mediate in the disputes of the Mansfeld counts. He writes six letters to K. on his way there. |
| 18th February 1546 | Luther dies in Eisleben. He is taken with a big escort via Halle to Wittenberg. |
| 22nd February 1546 | The funeral procession reaches Wittenberg, where Luther is buried in the castle church. Luther's will is |

not recognised by the legal profession. The Elector decides in favour of Katharina.

| | |
|---|---|
| November 1546 | K. flees from the emperor's army to Magdeburg. |
| April 1547 | K. flees to Braunschweig. |
| June 1547 | The family returns to Wittenberg. All the gardens are destroyed. |
| 1549 to 1551 | Hans studies law in Koenigsburg. His studies are paid for by Duke Albrecht. In Leipzig, K. is involved in many court proceedings regarding her claims on Zuelsdorf and amongst others against Marshall Hans Loeser. |
| 1551 or 52 | Hans marries Elisabeth Cruciger. |
| September 1552 | After several attacks of the Plague in the "black monastery" K starts out for Torgau together with Paul and Margarete. The horses bolt . K. falls and is injured. She is taken to Torgau. On her sickbed she keeps saying that she would like to hang like a "limpet" on the "robe" of Christ. |
| 20th December 1552 | K. dies in Torgau. She is buried in the city's church. |